Microwave Magic
Pasta and Rice

Grolier Limited
TORONTO

Contributors to this series:

Recipes and Technical Assistance:
École de cuisine Bachand-Bissonnette
Cooking consultants:
Denis Bissonette
Michèle Émond
Dietician:
Christiane Barbeau
Photos:
Laramée Morel Communications
Audio-Visuelles
Design:
Claudette Taillefer
Assistants:
Julie Deslauriers
Philippe O'Connor
Joan Pothier
Accessories:
Andrée Cournoyer
Writing:
Communications La Griffe Inc.
Text Consultants:
Cap et bc inc.
Advisors:
Roger Aubin
Joseph R. De Varennes
Gaston Lavoie
Kenneth H. Pearson

Assembly:
Carole Garon
Vital Lapalme
Jean-Pierre Larose
Carl Simmons
Gus Soriano
Marc Vallières
Production Managers:
Gilles Chamberland
Ernest Homewood
Production Assistants:
Martine Gingras
Catherine Gordon
Kathy Kishimoto
Peter Thomlison
Art Director:
Bernard Lamy
Editors:
Laurielle Ilacqua
Susan Marshall
Margaret Oliver
Robin Rivers
Lois Rock
Jocelyn Smyth
Donna Thomson
Dolores Williams
Development:
Le Groupe Polygone Éditeurs Inc.

We wish to thank the following firms, PIER I IMPORTS and LE CACHE POT, for their contribution to the illustration of this set.

The series editors have taken every care to ensure that the information given is accurate. However, no cookbook can guarantee the user successful results. The editors cannot accept any responsibility for the results obtained by following the recipes and recommendations given.

Canadian Cataloguing in Publication Data

Main entry under title:

Pasta and rice

(Microwave magic ; 12)
Translation of: Pâtes et riz.
Includes index.
ISBN 0-7172-2433-3

1. Cookery (Macaroni).   2. Cookery (Rice).   3. Microwave cookery.   I. Series: Microwave magic (Toronto, Ont.) ; 12.

TX832.P3813 1988   641.8'22   C88-094211-8

Contents

Note from the Editor 6

Power Levels 7

Pasta, Rice and the Microwave Oven 8

A Guide to Pasta 10

A Pasta Parade! 12

Utensils for Making Pasta 14

Utensils for Cooking Pasta 16

Storing Pasta 17

Cooking Pasta 18

Freezing and Defrosting Pasta 19

Spaghetti—A Universal Pasta 20

Pasta Recipes 22

Rice—An Underrated Staple 66

Rice Recipes 68

Entertaining 98

Pasta and Rice Terminology 106

Culinary Terms 108

Conversion Chart 109

Index 110

Microwave Magic is a multi-volume set, with each volume devoted to a particular type of cooking. So, if you are looking for a chicken recipe, you simply go to one of the two volumes that deal with poultry. Each volume has its own index, and the final volume contains a general index to the complete set.

Microwave Magic puts over twelve hundred recipes at your fingertips. You will find it as useful as the microwave oven itself. Enjoy!

Note from the Editor

How to Use this Book
The books in this set have been designed to make your job as easy as possible. As a result, most of the recipes are set out in a standard way.

We suggest that you begin by consulting the information chart for the recipe you have chosen. You will find there all the information you need to decide if you are able to make it: preparation time, cost per serving, level of difficulty, number of calories per serving and other relevant details. Thus, if you have only 30 minutes in which to prepare the evening meal, you will quickly be able to tell which recipe is possible and suits your schedule.

The list of ingredients is always clearly separated from the main text. When space allows, the ingredients are shown together in a photograph so that you can make sure you have them all without rereading the list—another way of saving your valuable time. In addition, for the more complex recipes we have supplied photographs of the key stages involved either in preparation or serving.

All the dishes in this book have been cooked in a 700 watt microwave oven. If your oven has a different wattage, consult the conversion chart that appears on the following page for cooking times in different types of oven. We would like to emphasize that the cooking times given in the book are a minimum. If a dish does not seem to be cooked enough, you may return it to the oven for a few more minutes. Also, the cooking time can vary according to your ingredients: their water and fat content, thickness, shape and even where they come from. We have therefore left a blank space on each recipe page in which you can note the cooking time that suits you best. This will enable you to add a personal touch to the recipes that we suggest and to reproduce your best results every time.

Although we have put all the technical information together at the front of this book, we have inserted a number of boxed entries called **MICROTIPS** throughout to explain particular techniques. They are brief and simple, and will help you obtain successful results in your cooking.

With the very first recipe you try, you will discover just how simple microwave cooking can be and how often it depends on techniques you already use for cooking with a conventional oven. If cooking is a pleasure for you, as it is for us, it will be all the more so with a microwave oven. Now let's get on with the food.

The Editor

Key to the Symbols
For ease of reference, the following symbols have been used on the recipe information charts.

The pencil symbol ✏ is a reminder to write your cooking time in the space provided.

Level of Difficulty

🍴 Easy

🍴🍴 Moderate

🍴🍴🍴 Complex

Cost per Serving

$ Inexpensive

$ $ Moderate

$ $ $ Expensive

Power Levels

All the recipes in this book have been tested in a 700 watt oven. As there are many microwave ovens on the market with different power levels, and as the names of these levels vary from one manufacturer to another, we have decided to give power levels as a percentage. To adapt the power levels given here, consult the chart opposite and the instruction manual for your oven.

Generally speaking, if you have a 500 watt or 600 watt oven you should increase cooking times by about 30% over those given, depending on the actual length of time required. The shorter the original cooking time, the greater the percentage by which it must be lengthened. The 30% figure is only an average. Consult the chart for detailed information on this topic.

Power Levels

HIGH: 100% - 90%	Vegetables (except boiled potatoes and carrots) Soup Sauce Fruits Browning ground beef Browning dish Popcorn
MEDIUM HIGH: 80% - 70%	Rapid defrosting of precooked dishes Muffins Some cakes Hot dogs
MEDIUM: 60% - 50%	Cooking tender meat Cakes Fish Seafood Eggs Reheating Boiled potatoes and carrots
MEDIUM LOW: 40%	Cooking less tender meat Simmering Melting chocolate
DEFROST: 30% **LOW: 30% - 20%**	Defrosting Simmering Cooking less tender meat
WARM: 10%	Keeping food warm Allowing yeast dough to rise

Cooking Time Conversion Chart

700 watts	600 watts*
5 s	11 s
15 s	20 s
30 s	40 s
45 s	1 min
1 min	1 min 20 s
2 min	2 min 40 s
3 min	4 min
4 min	5 min 20 s
5 min	6 min 40 s
6 min	8 min
7 min	9 min 20 s
8 min	10 min 40 s
9 min	12 min
10 min	13 min 30 s
20 min	26 min 40 s
30 min	40 min
40 min	53 min 40 s
50 min	66 min 40 s
1 h	1 h 20 min

* There is very little difference in cooking times between 500 watt ovens and 600 watt ovens.

Pasta, Rice and the Microwave Oven

In dedicating an entire volume of our Microwave Magic series to pasta and rice, we are drawing attention to the importance of the two major grain groups that nourish mankind: wheat, from which most types of pasta are made, and rice. Pasta and rice are certainly not new food discoveries, but the introduction of the microwave oven has provided new territory in which to explore new approaches to these well-known staples.

From Wheat to Pasta

We know that wheat has been cultivated for at least 10 000 years, but when and where the idea of transforming wheat into pasta first occurred to someone are less certain. It is probably reasonable to suppose that the invention of pasta is almost as old as the consumption of cooked wheat and that pasta was discovered simultaneously in various parts of the world. By observing the effects of the interaction between water and flour, ancient civilizations probably happened to produce the raw dough, later developing the idea of cooking it, and pasta was invented.

There has been considerable and still unresolved controversy surrounding the national origins of pasta, which are attributed to both China and Italy. We do know that "mian" noodles, which symbolized longevity, were consumed in China 3000 years before Christ. It is also known that Marco Polo brought the recipes for macaroni and won ton pasta back to Italy in the second half of the thirteenth century. This information would suggest that it was the Italians who imported and appropriated the use of pasta.

It should be noted, however, that pasta prepared in China was not all based on wheat—it was also made with rice, corn or peas. Nor was Chinese pasta prepared with sauces. The Italian method of preparing semolina-based pasta goes back to the Etruscans and the third century B.C. Certainly it was the Italians who enriched the modern repertoire of pastas and who developed the large variety of sauces that accompany it.

Rice: An Ancient Food

Rice is a grain that nourishes one third of humanity and is the basic food element throughout most of Asia. In fact, rice was first cultivated in this part of the world and Asia still produces most of the world's supply of rice. Its preparation and consumption has a long tradition; in China rice has been consumed for more than 5000 years.

While in the West we are familiar with a mere 50 different types of rice, although each type may well include several varieties, more than 7000 varieties are known in the Orient. Rice was imported to Europe by the Arabs in the Middle Ages and is now farmed on a large scale in North Carolina, but it has never enjoyed the same popularity in the West as it does in the Orient. In fact, rice has always remained in the shadow of wheat, our most basic food.

Today, the microwave oven opens new doors for the preparation of both pasta and rice. It not only simplifies traditional cooking methods, but also permits the application of new, more practical procedures with surprising results. We invite you to discover, with pleasure, two of our fundamental foods.

A Guide to Pasta

More than 80 different types of pasta are produced, so don't be surprised if you fail to recognize some of the more unusual shapes or if you have trouble visualizing exactly what new pasta discovery your friends may be trying to describe to you. In spite of the number of varieties produced, only a few of these different types of pasta may be found on the shelves of our local stores; because pasta is not a North American speciality, some of the less well-known types may not be widely distributed.

And to further complicate matters, there is a certain amount of confusion as to the names of some types of pasta. In fact, pasta made in Canada may have names that would not be recognized outside the country, and pasta produced in other countries may have names that have been adapted for their markets. Even in Italy the names of different varieties of pasta have not been standardized and vary from region to region. For example, the pasta known as *fettuccine* in the region of Rome is called *tagliatelle* in other parts of Italy. Likewise, the wider noodles are variously called *fettucce* and *tagliatelle larghe*.

Rather than provide an exhaustive list of the many different types of pasta, we offer the following basic guide which will help you not only to attain a better understanding of the varieties you encounter on restaurant menus, but also to shop for the right kind of pasta when you choose a recipe from this book.

Fresh Pasta and Dried Pasta

To begin with, pasta can be divided into two distinct categories—fresh and dried. Much of the pasta that is cut into ribbons, such as fettuccine and linguine, as well as most filled pasta, such as ravioli and tortellini, belong to the first category. Fresh or homemade pasta is usually made with all-purpose flour and eggs and is traditionally associated with the dishes of northern Italy. Dried or commercially produced pasta, such as spaghetti and macaroni, is made with semolina (milled from hard durum wheat) and water, resulting in a stronger pasta to withstand the handling involved in packaging and shipping. Dishes prepared with dried pasta are generally associated with southern Italian cuisine.

Most types of pasta, including spaghetti, can be bought fresh these days, but dried pasta is undoubtedly more convenient and the majority is sold this way. The delicacy and the quality of the flavor depend, of course, on the ingredients used. Pasta made with hard wheat flour is firmer than that made with mixed flour or soft wheat flour.

Pasta Grouped by Shape

Pasta is one food in which shape plays an important role. Indeed, what other characteristic distinguishes lasagna from cannelloni when the recipe for the pasta dough is identical? Here, we identify several types of pasta, grouped according to shape and size.

1. Pasta Cut into Ribbons

This group refers to pasta that is cut into long, flat ribbons and includes, from wide to narrow: lasagna and scalloped lasagna; lasagnette and scalloped lasagnette; mafalda, or narrow lasagnette with 45° scallops; yolanda, narrow strips of pasta scalloped on one side only; fettucce or tagliatelle larghe, flat narrow ribbons but wider than fettuccine; and finally, tagliatelle or fettuccine, very narrow ribbons of pasta.

2. Pasta Cut into Sections

This group is composed of varying widths of tubular pasta cut into different lengths and, from large to small, includes: tufoli, large rigatoni with a smooth surface; rigatoni, a well-known curved pasta scored with grooves; penne, long sections of macaroni cut on the bias and resembling quill pens; cornets, or short sections of macaroni less curved than elbows; elbows, short curved pasta tubes; and ditalini, very short sections of wide macaroni resembling rings or thimbles.

3. The Macaroni Family

The macaroni family includes only pasta with a long, straight tubular form. If the tubes are cut into sections or are curved, their names change and they belong to other categories. Macaroni is produced in varying sizes, from broad round strips to those that are very fine.

4. The Spaghetti Family

Long, cylindrical strips of pasta belong to the spaghetti family and include: spaghetti (round thin strips), spaghettini (small spaghetti), vermicelli (tiny spaghetti strips, translating as "little worms") and angel's hair (very fine strips).

5. Filled Pasta

As the name indicates, the pasta in this category always contains a filling and includes: agnolotti, a semi-circular turnover with scalloped edges; ravioli, or small squares; cannelloni, a wide, straight tubular pasta similar to rigatoni; manicotti, or large cannelloni, grooved and cut on the bias; and tortellini, which are small crescents.

6. Soup Pasta

This category includes a multitude of small pasta shapes used in soups. Named according to their shape, these include alphabets, rings, coils, curled shells, stars, pearls, wagon wheels, and many others. Obviously, a number of these pasta shapes could be used in a decorative capacity as well.

7. Decorative Pasta

This group of fancy pasta shapes, some too large to be used in soups, includes "small hats," large and small shells, little pipes, corkscrews, spirals, and a number of pasta shapes described as soup pasta.

We should also mention that pasta from the spaghetti family as well as pasta cut into ribbons is not always packaged straight and flat but may be folded in two or rolled up into a sort of nest. Chinese noodles are frequently pressed into a block to be packaged.

A Pasta Parade!

1. **Pasta Cut into Ribbons**
   A - Scalloped lasagna
   B - Lasagna
   C - Scalloped lasagnette
   D - Mafalda
   E - Fettuccine
   F - Linguine

G - Tagliatelle (in nests)
H - Yolanda

2. **Pasta Cut into Sections**
   A - Elbows
   B - Cornets
   C - Penne (quill pens)

D - Ditalini (rings or thimbles)
E - Pennini (little quill pens)
F - Rigatoni

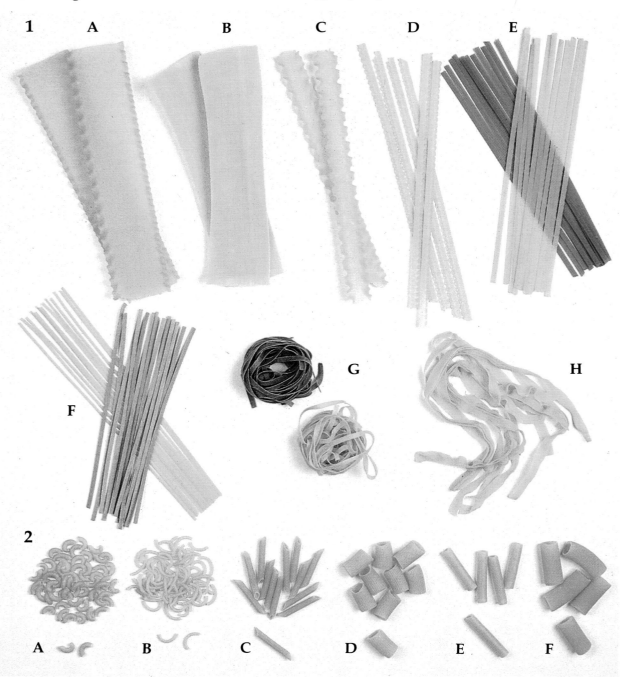

3. **The Macaroni Family**
   A - very fine
   B - fine
   C - moderately broad
   D - broad

4. **The Spaghetti Family**
   A - Vermicelli
   B - Spaghettini
   C - Spinach spaghetti
   D - Spaghetti

5. **Filled Pasta**
   A - Manicotti
   B - Cannelloni
   C - Ravioli
   D - Shells
   E - Tortellini

6. **Soup Pasta**
   A - Tiny bows
   B - Stars
   C - Orzo   D - Tiny rings
   E - Wagon wheels

F - Little pipes
G - Butterflies

7. **Decorative Pasta**
   A - Small squares
   B - Pearls
   C - Small hats
   D - Little curls
   E - Corkscrews
   F - Large and small
       conch shells
   G - Spirals or twists

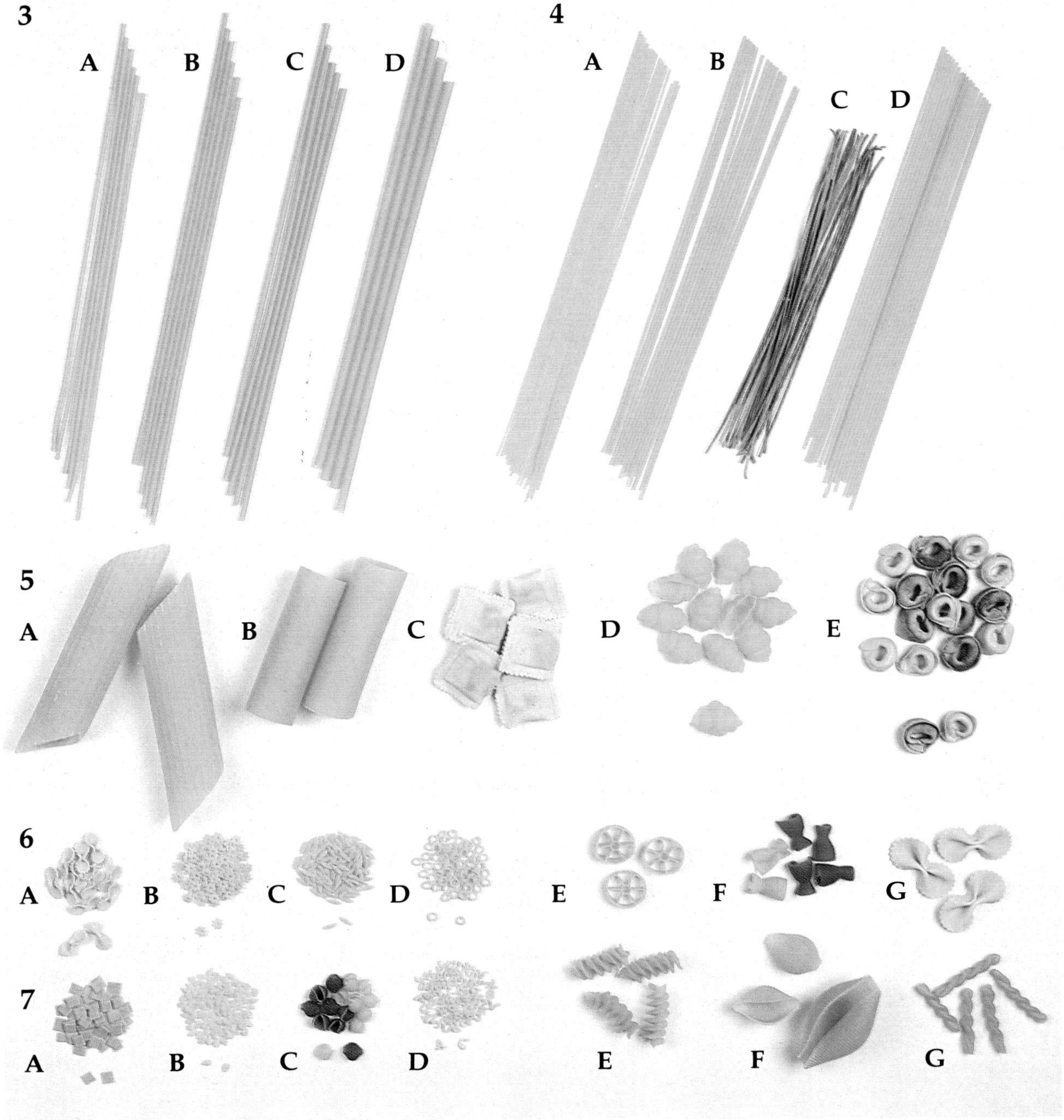

3

A   B   C   D

4

A   B   C   D

5

A   B   C   D   E

6

A   B   C   D   E   F   G

7

A   B   C   D   E   F   G

13

Utensils for Making Pasta

Numerous sophisticated utensils and machines are available for those who enjoy making pasta at home. Each is designed for a specific purpose and, therefore, not all are necessary for your first experiments. Before buying any equipment, consider what kind of pasta you would like to make and buy only what is needed for that. If you find that you really enjoy making pasta, you can then complete your collection of utensils and make all the different kinds of pasta at home.

The Basic Pasta Machine
The pasta machine is the basic tool for the preparation of all recipes based on long, flat sheets of pasta. Equipped with two rollers and a handle crank, the distance between the rollers is adjustable so that the pasta can be passed through the rollers several times, producing very thin sheets. More complex models come equipped with different sized cutters, which slice the dough into varying widths (from broad lasagna noodles to very fine tagliatelle).

Specialized Pasta Machines
A specialized pasta machine is used to make pasta shaped into shells, which may then be filled. An electric extrusion machine that is capable of producing cylindrical strips of pasta belonging to the spaghetti and macaroni families is also available.

The Rolling Pin
The regular rolling pin can be used in place of the pasta machine to roll out the dough. It is also used to roll the dough into pasta molds.

The Ravioli Mold
Used to assemble the ravioli, the first layer of dough is placed on the mold, the filling is added to the center of the squares, and the second layer of dough is placed on top to seal the ravioli.

The Ravioli Rolling Pin
This rolling pin is used to cut the filled ravioli dough into regular square shapes. It is very helpful in making ravioli if a mold is not used.

The Ravioli Wheel
Ravioli wheels are also available in different sizes to cut the filled ravioli dough into regular square shapes.

The Ravioli Cutter
This functions like a cookie or donut cutter and enables you to cut the ravioli squares, one by one, so that the edges are scalloped.

The Agnolotti Wheel
This wheel, like the ravioli wheel, is used to cut the filled dough into the desired shape —in this case, into circles.

The Agnolotti Cutter
This cutter serves the same purpose as the agnolotti wheel, but like the ravioli cutter, it produces scalloped edges.

The Pastry Wheel
This is a fluted wheel that is very useful for cutting thin layers of pasta dough without ripping it.

Cannelloni Tubes
These tubes are used only by those who are extremely dedicated to making cannelloni at home.

Utensils for Cooking Pasta

Only a few years ago, before the introduction of the microwave oven, there was only one way to cook pasta—and that was to boil a pot of water on top of the stove and add the pasta. With this method the pasta that was too long for the pot remained half immersed in water until it softened enough to be pushed completely into the pot with a fork. The microwave oven eliminates this problem; long pasta can be cooked in long, shallow dishes to ensure uniform cooking.

Avoid Metal!

When selecting a container to cook any type of pasta, always remember the effect of metal on microwaves. The oven emits microwaves, which are absorbed by the molecules in foods, thus creating internal heat. This interaction occurs only when the waves can travel freely through the container holding the food. Metal containers deflect these waves and thus cannot be used for microwave cooking.

Choosing a Cooking Dish

Since pasta is always cooked in boiling water, the container used must be heat resistant. The ideal container is a transparent glass dish with a cover, or with edges so that it can be covered with plastic wrap. Covering the dish during exposure to the microwaves prevents the water from splattering the inside of the oven. Whatever container is used, however, it should be large enough to have the pasta completely immersed in the water throughout the cooking time.

A 2 liter (8 cup) glass container is best for cooking any pasta cut into short lengths. This size will accommodate a good quantity of pasta—at least 225 g (8 oz). A 1 liter (4 cup) dish is suitable for smaller pasta shapes, such as penne, rings or ravioli.

Smaller quantities of pasta require less water, less time and less power. To cook long varieties of pasta, such as lasagna, spaghetti and other such pastas, a large glass 30 x 20 x 5 cm (12 x 8 x 2 in) baking dish is ideal because it permits the total immersion of the pasta in water from the beginning of the cooking time. Just make sure that the dish can be covered with plastic wrap. Other dishes, for example, any square or round dishes with adequate capacity, are also suitable for cooking most types of pasta, except long pasta. Always remember, however, that the dish used should not be filled to capacity.

Storing Pasta

Most people do not give a great deal of thought to storing dried, uncooked pasta. As long as the pasta is kept dust free, it is generally thought that it will remain savory and nourishing for an indefinite period of time. Storing pasta, however, does require some care.

Dried Pasta

Dried pasta accounts for more than 90% of the pasta sold on the market and has approximately the same nutritional value as fresh pasta. Industrially produced pasta is enriched to mitigate the loss of nutritional elements during the production process. While dried pasta is the easiest pasta to store, its nutritional elements are nonetheless not eternal. Most pasta, stored in ideal conditions, begins to lose its nutritional value after 6 months. Dried pasta containing egg or vegetables will last for less time.

And what conditions are ideal for storing dried pasta? First, the location must be cool and dry because vitamins are sensitive to heat and humidity. This fact also means that the pasta should not be exposed to sunlight. Many people neglect this requirement, storing their pasta in a variety of decorative transparent cannisters on kitchen countertops. And, of course, pasta should also be stored in containers that can be hermetically sealed.

Consequently, if dried pasta is to be stored on open shelves or on the countertop, it should be placed in opaque containers. If stored in a cool kitchen cupboard or pantry, it should be placed in hermetically sealed polyethylene bags or in other containers that are airtight.

Fresh Pasta

Although the nutritional value of fresh pasta is not any higher than that of dried pasta, fresh pasta definitely has more flavor. Whether you make it yourself or buy it, fresh pasta should be consumed as quickly as possible. If needed, it can be stored in an airtight polyethylene bag in the refrigerator for about two weeks. Pasta made with vegetables will last less time.

Cooked Pasta

Extra or leftover pasta is easy to reheat in the microwave oven. In fact, interestingly enough, the flavor of some pasta dishes prepared with tomato or meat sauce is actually enhanced on reheating.

If the pasta has been combined with other ingredients, the length of time it can be safely stored will depend on these ingredients. For example, pasta prepared with egg or seafood will keep much less time than pasta prepared with a meatless tomato sauce. Pasta that has been cooked only in boiling water can be kept for about 3 days; placing a moist towel over it will help prevent it from drying out. Cooked pasta tends to dry out quickly and should always be stored in airtight containers or in dishes covered with plastic wrap.

Cooking Pasta

Pasta cooks as well in the microwave oven as it does on the stove and, in fact, the microwave oven offers certain distinct advantages. With a microwave oven, pasta can be cooked in shallow rectangular dishes, which allow long pasta such as lasagna and spaghetti to be evenly cooked without boiling large amounts of water. A further advantage is that the microwaves pass through the cooking dish without warming it so that the pasta does not stick to the dish in which it is cooked.

Rules to Follow

Certain basic rules apply to cooking pasta, as they do to cooking any other food. But pasta really is very easy to cook if these simple rules are observed.

The type of cooking dish used depends on the type and amount of pasta to be cooked. Shallow rectangular baking dishes made of glass are best for long pasta, while deeper round dishes are suitable for other types (see the section on cooking utensils on page 16). The dish should be large enough to hold the pasta and the water without being more than three-quarters full.

When cooking pasta in the microwave oven, don't use too much water; pasta contains hydrosoluble vitamins which would tend to be diluted. On the other hand, enough water must be used to allow the pasta to move freely without sticking together, as the water boils. It is also important to remember that pasta will double in volume as it cooks.

The first step in cooking pasta in the microwave oven is the same as that in traditional cooking—bringing water to the boil. When the water in the microwave reaches the boiling point, quickly add all the pasta and put it back into the oven so that the water reaches the boiling point again as quickly as possible. The water should boil continuously during the cooking time. Cover the container to prevent the water from splashing the inside of the oven. If using plastic wrap to cover the dish, pierce it in 2 or 3 places to allow for the release of steam.

Use a wooden spoon to stir the pasta once halfway through the cooking time. When the pasta is done to your liking, pour it into a colander, drain and rinse under cold water.

Checking for Doneness

The best way to check whether pasta is done to your satisfaction is to taste it. Like vegetables, pasta is best if somewhat underdone. Italians call this *al dente*. This expression translates as "to the tooth," meaning that the pasta should be firm enough to yield only to the teeth and not to the tongue.

Freezing and Defrosting Pasta

The Whys and Hows of Freezing

With its unique feature of defrosting food quickly without beginning the cooking process, the microwave oven allows you to take advantage of the time you have available for cooking. For this reason, it is a good idea to double your recipe and freeze half for future use.

Cooking dishes can be frozen, but some keep less well in the freezer than others. Pasta dishes prepared with seafood or egg-based sauces, for instance, keep for less time than those with a simple tomato sauce. However, because all pasta can be successfully reheated in the microwave oven and because pasta retains its nutritional qualities when defrosted, it is a good idea to take advantage of the opportunity of freezing it. In fact, many connoisseurs agree that some pasta dishes, such as lasagna and other preparations with plenty of tomato sauce, taste better when reheated.

As with any other food to be frozen, pasta should be well sealed to protect it from the cold dry air of the freezer. Choose solid airtight containers rather than dishes covered with plastic wrap. Round microwave-safe dishes are best because they can be taken from the freezer and put directly into the microwave, and the round shape will ensure a uniform distribution of the microwaves during defrosting and reheating.

The length of time that pasta dishes can be stored in the freezer depends on the ingredients used. For example, lasagna made with a meat and tomato sauce will still be tasty after 6 to 8 weeks in the freezer.

Defrosting Pasta

For the amount of time needed to defrost pasta, consult the above chart which gives, first, the defrosting times for cooked pasta without sauce and, second, the times for prepared pasta dishes.

The microwave should be set at 70% power for defrosting all pasta, and the defrosting time will naturally vary according to quantity. The figures shown in the chart all refer to 115 g (4 oz) servings.

Defrosting Times for Pasta, by Type and Number of Servings (at 70%)

Pasta Without Sauce	1 Serving	2 Servings	3 Servings
Lasagna	4 min	6 min	8 min
Spaghetti	3 min	5 min	7 min
Small unfilled pasta	3 min	5 min	7 min
Filled ravioli and tortellini	4 min	6 min	8 min
Prepared Pasta	**1 Serving**	**2 Servings**	**3 Servings**
Cannelloni	5 min	7 min	9 min
Lasagna	5 min	7 min	9 min
Spaghetti with sauce	5 min	7 min	9 min
Small unfilled pasta in sauce	4 min	6 min	8 min
Ravioli and tortellini	5 min	7 min	9 min

Spaghetti—A Universal Pasta

There is little doubt that spaghetti is the most popular type of pasta among North Americans. In spite of its very long tradition, we do not know a great deal about the origins of this particular form of pasta, though it is generally believed to have been invented in Naples. There is no mystery, however, about the derivation of the word itself. The long, narrow, cylindrical shape of the pasta is similar in appearance to string, or *spago* in Italian. Hence, *spaghetti,* or "little string," the name by which this particular form of pasta is universally known.

The popularity of spaghetti prepared with sauce spread from Naples to the whole of Italy and particularly to the areas of Liguria and Rome. Spaghetti was always made at home prior to the Renaissance, when commercial production of spaghetti and macaroni began. It was at that time that spaghetti began to gain in popularity throughout the world.

The Spaghetti Family

Spaghetti, in terms of width and sometimes length, is the largest member of its family. Next comes spaghettini, a little thinner than spaghetti and often mistaken for it. Spaghettini is also sometimes called linguettine. Vermicelli is even finer than spaghettini and is usually prepared differently. It is often fried when used in traditional Chinese dishes but Western cuisine uses it, whole or cut into shorter lengths, in soups and with seafood sauces. Finally, angel's hair is the most narrow pasta of the spaghetti family. It is available loosely rolled into small nests.

All these different members of the spaghetti family can be prepared in a number of delicious ways.

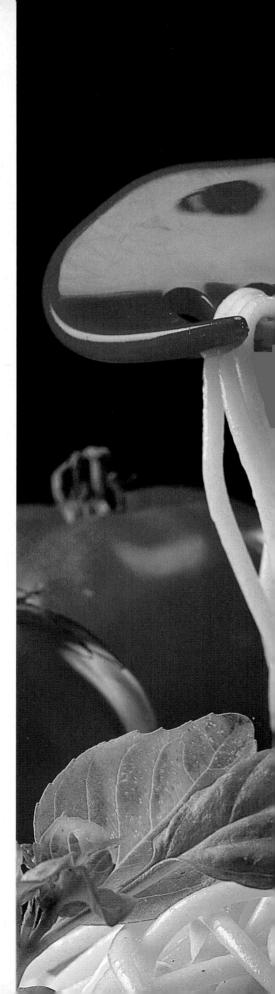

Spaghetti with Meatballs and Tomato Sauce

Level of Difficulty	¶¶¶
Preparation Time	25 min
Cost per Serving	$
Number of Servings	8
Nutritional Value	422 calories 30.3 g protein 40.5 g carbohydrate
Food Exchanges	3 oz meat 2 vegetable exchanges 2 bread exchanges
Cooking Time	45 min
Standing Time	None
Power Level	100%, 90%
Write Your Cooking Time Here	

Ingredients

450 g (1 lb) spaghetti
1 L (4 cups) water
5 mL (1 teaspoon) oil
5 mL (1 teaspoon) salt

Tomato Sauce:
30 mL (2 tablespoons) oil
125 mL (1/2 cup) onion, chopped
4 cloves garlic, crushed
1 398 mL (14 oz) can tomatoes, crushed
75 mL (1/3 cup) tomato paste
7 mL (1-1/2 teaspoons) oregano

2 mL (1/2 teaspoon) basil
1 bay leaf
5 mL (1 teaspoon) sugar
15 mL (1 tablespoon) crushed chili peppers
30 mL (2 tablespoons) Worcestershire sauce

Meatballs:
900 g (2 lb) minced veal
50 mL (1/4 cup) Italian breadcrumbs
1 clove garlic, crushed
10 mL (2 teaspoons) sweet mustard
pepper to taste

Method

— First prepare the sauce by combining the oil, onion and 4 crushed cloves of garlic in a baking dish; cook at 100% for 3 minutes, stirring once during the cooking time.
— Add the tomatoes, tomato paste, oregano, basil, bay leaf, sugar, chili peppers and Worcestershire sauce, and cook uncovered at 100% for 11 minutes, stirring twice during the cooking time. Set aside.

— While the sauce cooks, combine the minced veal, breadcrumbs, garlic, mustard and pepper in a bowl. Mix well.
— Shape the mixture into small meatballs and cook on a bacon rack at 90% for 9 to 11 minutes, or until the meat is cooked, giving the dish a half-turn twice during the cooking time. Add the meatballs to the tomato sauce.
— To prepare the pasta, pour the water into a large rectangular baking dish and bring to the boil by heating at 100% for about 10 minutes.
— Add the oil and salt and the spaghetti; cover and cook at 100% for 9 to 10 minutes, stirring every 3 minutes.
— Drain the cooked pasta; reheat the tomato sauce and the meatballs and pour over the spaghetti.

Shape the meat mixture into small meatballs, place them on a bacon rack, and cook at 90% for 9 to 11 minutes.

Spaghetti Carbonara

Level of Difficulty	🍴🍴
Preparation Time	15 min
Cost per Serving	$
Number of Servings	4
Nutritional Value	542 calories 22 g protein 33.7 g carbohydrate
Food Exchanges	2 oz meat 2 bread exchanges 4 fat exchanges
Cooking Time	33 min
Standing Time	None
Power Level	100%, 70%
Write Your Cooking Time Here	

Ingredients
225 g (8 oz) spaghetti
1 L (4 cups) water
5 mL (1 teaspoon) oil
5 mL (1 teaspoon) salt
10 slices of bacon

Sauce:
3 eggs, beaten
50 mL (1/4 cup) 35% cream
45 mL (3 tablespoons) butter
175 mL (3/4 cup) Parmesan
cheese, grated
salt and pepper to taste

Method
— To prepare the pasta, pour the water into a large rectangular baking dish, cover and bring to the boil by heating at 100% for 10 minutes.
— Add the oil, salt and pasta and cook at 100% for 7 to 9 minutes, stirring every 3 minutes. Rinse the pasta under cold water and set aside.
— Place the bacon strips on a rack, cover with paper towel to prevent splattering, and cook at 100% for 8 to 10 minutes or until the bacon is crispy; crumble the bacon and set aside.
— To prepare the sauce, combine the beaten eggs with the cream and set aside.
— Melt the butter in a dish at 100% for 1 minute, add the Parmesan cheese and mix well, and then add the eggs and cream mixture. Season to taste.
— In a casserole, combine the sauce with the crumbled bacon and the cooked

spaghetti; stir to distribute the sauce and the bacon evenly, and heat at 70% for 2 to 3 minutes before serving.

Stir the spaghetti frequently during the cooking time to prevent the strands from sticking together.

Place the bacon slices on a rack, cover with paper towel to prevent splattering, and cook as directed.

Spaghettini with Clam Sauce

Level of Difficulty	
Preparation Time	15 min
Cost per Serving	$
Number of Servings	8
Nutritional Value	226 calories 14 g protein 38 g carbohydrate
Food Exchanges	1 oz meat 1 vegetable exchange 2 bread exchanges
Cooking Time	29 min
Standing Time	None
Power Level	100%
Write Your Cooking Time Here	

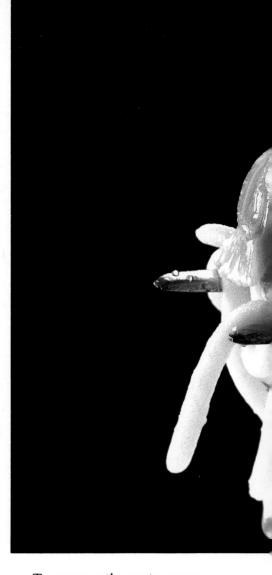

Ingredients
450 g (1 lb) spaghettini
1 L (4 cups) water
5 mL (1 teaspoon) oil
5 mL (1 teaspoon) salt

Sauce:
2 426 mL (15 oz) cans of clams
2 cloves garlic, crushed
1 796 mL (28 oz) can of tomatoes, chopped
30 mL (2 tablespoons) parsley, chopped
salt and pepper to taste

Method
— To prepare the sauce, drain the clams and strain the liquid through a sieve; set the clams aside.
— Combine the clam liquid, garlic, tomatoes, parsley, salt and pepper and mix well; cook at 100% for 4 to 5 minutes, stirring once during the cooking time.
— Break up the tomatoes with a fork and add the clams.
— Continue to cook at 100% for 5 to 6 minutes, stirring twice during the cooking time. Set aside.
— To prepare the pasta, pour the water into a rectangular baking dish and bring to the boil by heating at 100% for 6 to 9 minutes; add the oil, salt and spaghettini and cover with plastic wrap.
— Cook at 100% for 6 to 9 minutes, stirring every 3 minutes.
— Drain the cooked pasta.
— Reheat the sauce, pour over the spaghettini and serve immediately.

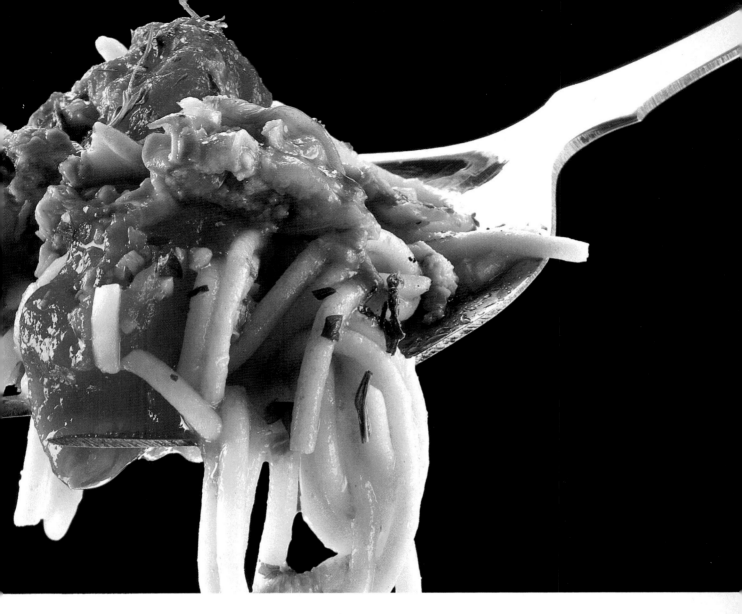

Assemble the ingredients required to make this exquisite sauce.

Put the spaghettini in the boiling water, cover with plastic wrap and cook as directed.

MICROTIPS

Use Cheese Instead of Butter and Salt

Pasta should not be overseasoned. The addition of salt and butter may be avoided if you are preparing pasta with cheese—the cheese contains enough fat and salt to season the dish. This suggestion should make calorie counters happy!

Spaghetti with Tuna Sauce

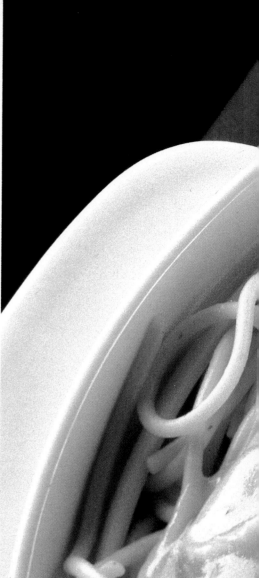

Level of Difficulty	🍴
Preparation Time	15 min
Cost per Serving	**$**
Number of Servings	6
Nutritional Value	337 calories 16.6 g protein 40.4 g carbohydrate
Food Exchanges	1-1/2 oz meat 2-1/2 bread exchanges 1 fat exchange
Cooking Time	29 min
Standing Time	None
Power Level	100%
Write Your Cooking Time Here	

Ingredients
450 g (1 lb) spaghetti
1 L (4 cups) water
5 mL (1 teaspoon) oil
5 mL (1 teaspoon) salt

Sauce:
1 clove garlic, crushed
30 mL (2 tablespoons) butter
30 mL (2 tablespoons) parsley, chopped
250 mL (1 cup) chicken stock
250 mL (1 cup) tuna, flaked
15 mL (1 tablespoon) cornstarch
30 mL (2 tablespoons) water

Method
— To prepare the sauce, put the garlic and butter in a baking dish and cook at 100% for 2 minutes, stirring once during the cooking time.
— Add the parsley, continue to cook at 100% for 1 minute and then add the chicken stock and the tuna; cover and cook at 100% for 3 to 4 minutes or until the mixture is very hot, stirring once during the cooking time.
— Dissolve the cornstarch in the water and add it to the sauce; cook at 100% for 2 to 3 minutes, stirring every minute; set aside.
— To prepare the pasta, pour 1 L (4 cups) of water into a large baking dish and bring to the boil by heating at 100% for 8 to 10 minutes.
— Add the oil, salt and the pasta and cook at 100% for 6 to 9 minutes, stirring twice during the cooking time.
— Drain the cooked pasta and reheat the sauce; pour over the spaghetti and serve immediately.

These are the ingredients needed for this very original pasta recipe.

Add the flaked tuna to the garlic, butter, parsley and chicken stock and cook at 100% for 3 to 4 minutes.

Add the dissolved cornstarch to the sauce to thicken it.

Spaghettini with Garlic

Level of Difficulty	⑪
Preparation Time	10 min
Cost per Serving	$
Number of Servings	8
Nutritional Value	300 calories 6 g protein 32.5 g carbohydrate
Food Exchanges	2 bread exchanges 3-1/2 fat exchanges
Cooking Time	21 min
Standing Time	None
Power Level	100%
Write Your Cooking Time Here	

Ingredients
450 g (1 lb) spaghettini
1 L (4 cups) water
5 mL (1 teaspoon) oil
5 mL (1 teaspoon) salt

Sauce:
125 mL (1/2 cup) olive oil
4 cloves garlic, crushed
50 mL (1/4 cup) Parmesan
cheese, grated

Method
— To prepare the pasta, pour
the water into a large
baking dish and bring to
the boil by heating at
100% for about 10
minutes.
— Add the oil, salt and
spaghettini and cook at
100% for 6 to 9 minutes
or until done, stirring
twice during the cooking
time.
— Drain the cooked pasta
and set aside.
— To prepare the sauce, put
the olive oil and garlic in a
large dish and heat at
100% for 2 minutes,
stirring once during the
cooking time.
— Add the cooked
spaghettini to the dish and
stir well to coat evenly
with the garlic and oil.
— Garnish with grated
Parmesan cheese and
serve immediately.

MICROTIPS

Pasta and Cheese

It has become so customary to serve spaghetti with grated Parmesan cheese that we tend to take this garnish for granted. In fact, the use of cheese with pasta is a tradition that dates from ancient Rome. While Italians have used grated Parmesan as a condiment for centuries, it is only in the last few decades that we have begun to do the same.

The types of cheeses that can be used with pasta can be divided into two groups: hard and soft. Hard cheeses are granular and, because they can be finely grated, they are also more decorative than soft cheeses. Their flavor is usually quite pronounced —sometimes, even sharp. Parmesan is probably one of the best examples of a hard cheese with these qualities. Soft cheeses, such as mozzarella, may also be grated or shredded but tend to fall in larger chunks, melting in contact with heat to give the dish a smooth, soft texture.

Lasagna

Everyone is familiar with the taste and look of lasagna—it undoubtedly runs a close second to spaghetti in terms of reputation and popularity.

It is easy to lose sight of the fact that lasagna is not a separate type of pasta and that, like spaghetti or macaroni, it is part of a broader group—in this case, the pasta family that is cut into long, flat ribbons from sheets of rolled out dough. This group includes flat lasagna, sometimes very wide, and lasagna with scalloped edges as well as the narrower lasagnette and mafalda. Other types of pasta cut into ribbons, such as yolanda and fettuccine, are much narrower and are used in a different way.

The flavor of the pasta dough used for lasagna can vary widely. The addition of spinach juice to the dough is a classic recipe but only one of many possible ways of altering the flavor. For one thing, the taste of spinach can be further accentuated by adding the spinach itself, cooked, drained and finely chopped, instead of merely adding the juice.

As well, many other vegetables prepared in the same way (cooked, drained and finely chopped) can be used instead of spinach. Lasagna dough made with tomatoes, fresh or dried herbs or pistachios—to mention just a few possibilities—combines well with most sauces and garnishes. The final dish will delight the eye as well as the taste buds.

There is one aspect of lasagna that is often ignored—and that is the decorative potential it offers. Perhaps because lasagna noodles are traditionally buried under cheese and tomato sauce, it does not occur to us that they can be used to decorate other dishes. But in actual fact, they make a unique and creative garnish for a number of dishes in a number of ways.

Lasagna noodles can be cut into small or large squares, their edges tailored to form attractive scallops. The long, narrower lasagnette noodles, without scallops, can be tied into loops or knots. Many noodles from this family may be shaped into a crown and used to hold other pasta preparations, or they may be coiled over cheese around the edge of a serving platter.

In effect, the number of ways in which this pasta can add flair to the presentation of food is endless. Let your imagination go wild!

Classic Lasagna

Level of Difficulty	
Preparation Time	20 min
Cost per Serving	$
Number of Servings	8
Nutritional Value	346 calories 24.8 g protein 34 g carbohydrate
Food Exchanges	3 oz meat 1/2 vegetable exchange 1-1/2 bread exchanges
Cooking Time	30 min
Standing Time	None
Power Level	100%, 70%
Write Your Cooking Time Here	

Ingredients
340 g (12 oz) lasagna
1 L (4 cups) water
5 mL (1 teaspoon) oil
5 mL (1 teaspoon) salt

Filling:
750 mL (3 cups) prepared
Italian-style meat sauce
340 g (12 oz) cottage cheese
115 g (4 oz) Parmesan cheese,
grated
250 mL (1 cup) mozzarella
cheese, grated
paprika to garnish

Method
— To prepare the lasagna, pour the water into a rectangular baking dish and cover with plastic wrap; bring to the boil by heating at 100% for 8 to 10 minutes.
— Add the oil, salt and the lasagna, arranging the noodles so that they are standing on edge in parallel rows; cook at 100% for 8 to 10 minutes, detaching the strips from one another halfway through the cooking time.
— Drain the cooked lasagna, rinse under cold water and set aside.
— Arrange one layer of lasagna in the bottom of the baking dish and cover with half the meat sauce, cottage cheese and Parmesan.
— Place another layer of lasagna in the dish and cover with the remaining meat sauce, cottage cheese and Parmesan.
— Top the ingredients with the grated mozzarella cheese and sprinkle with paprika.
— Cook, uncovered, at 70% for 8 to 10 minutes, giving the dish a half-turn halfway through the cooking time.

Lasagna is always suitable, whether for a small party or for a family supper. These are the ingredients you will need for its preparation.

Put the lasagna into the boiling water, arranging the noodles on edge in parallel rows.

Garnish the assembled dish with paprika before placing it in the oven.

35

Spinach Lasagna Bolognese

Level of Difficulty	🍴🍴
Preparation Time	25 min
Cost per Serving	**$**
Number of Servings	10
Nutritional Value	525 calories 26.6 g protein 59.6 g carbohydrate
Food Exchanges	2-1/2 oz meat 1 vegetable exchange 1 fat exchange 3 bread exchanges 1/2 milk exchange
Cooking Time	1 h 18 min
Standing Time	None
Power Level	100%, 70%
Write Your Cooking Time Here	

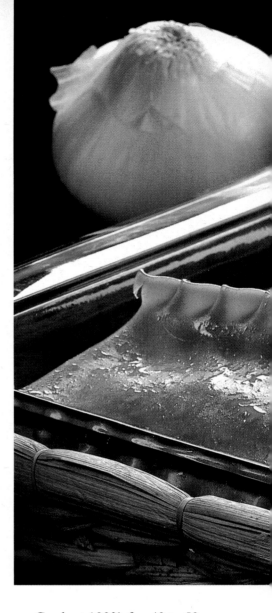

Ingredients
900 g (2 lb) spinach lasagna, cooked
125 mL (1/2 cup) Parmesan cheese, grated
paprika to garnish

Bolognese Sauce:
450 g (1 lb) ground beef
340 g (12 oz) prosciutto ham, minced
1 celery stalk, diced
1 onion, finely chopped
1 carrot, grated
2 341 mL (12 oz) cans tomatoes, chopped
250 mL (1 cup) chicken stock

Béchamel Sauce:
50 mL (1/4 cup) butter
50 mL (1/4 cup) flour
500 mL (2 cups) milk
salt and pepper to taste

Method
— To prepare the bolognese sauce, combine the ground beef and the prosciutto in a dish and cook at 100% for 4 to 6 minutes, stirring twice with a fork to break up the meat during the cooking time; set aside.
— Place all the vegetables in a baking dish and pour in 125 mL (1/2 cup) of the chicken stock; cover and cook at 100% for 3 to 5 minutes, stirring once during the cooking time.
— Add the remaining chicken stock and the cooked meat to the vegetables and mix well.
— Cook at 100% for 40 to 50 minutes, stirring three times during the cooking time; set aside.
— To prepare the béchamel sauce, put the butter in a dish and heat at 100% for 1 minute.
— Add the flour and mix well.
— Add the milk, beating with a wire whisk, and season.
— Cook the béchamel sauce at 100% for 5 to 7 minutes, stirring every 2 minutes; set aside.
— Spoon some of the

bolognese sauce into a rectangular dish, cover with a layer of lasagna, and add half the béchamel sauce.
— Add another layer of pasta; cover with some of the bolognese sauce and then with béchamel.
— Continue to alternate the layers, until all the ingredients are used, finishing with a layer of béchamel sauce.
— Sprinkle the assembled dish with the Parmesan and the paprika.

— Cook uncovered at 70% for 7 to 9 minutes or until the dish is hot.

This is a tasty and substantial dish, one that will be enjoyed by everyone. Make sure you have all the ingredients you need before beginning the recipe.

Lasagna with Four Cheeses

Level of Difficulty	🍴🍴
Preparation Time	20 min
Cost per Serving	**$**
Number of Servings	4
Nutritional Value	390 calories 26.8 g protein 50.3 g carbohydrate
Food Exchanges	2-1/2 oz meat 3 bread exchanges 1/2 milk exchange
Cooking Time	31 min
Standing Time	None
Power Level	100%, 70%
Write Your Cooking Time Here	

MICROTIPS

Which Cheese to Choose?

For spaghetti, macaroni and most filled pasta, Parmesan cheese is always appropriate. Mozzarella adds richness to macaroni and rigatoni. Ricotta is often used as a filling for pasta shells but can also be used as a garnish for spaghetti. It should be noted, however, that Italian cheeses are not the only ones that can be used in pasta dishes—for example, Gruyère or Emmenthal are delicious with tagliatelle or fettuccine.

Ingredients

340 g (12 oz) lasagna
1 L (4 cups) water
5 mL (1 teaspoon) oil
5 mL (1 teaspoon) salt

Filling:
75 mL (1/3 cup) provolone cheese, sliced
75 mL (1/3 cup) Gruyère cheese, sliced
150 mL (2/3 cup) mozzarella cheese, grated
75 mL (1/3 cup) Parmesan cheese, grated
paprika to garnish

Method

— To prepare the pasta, pour the water into a rectangular baking dish and bring to the boil by heating at 100% for 8 to 10 minutes; add the oil, salt and the lasagna and cover with plastic wrap.
— Cook at 100% for 8 to 10 minutes, gently stirring halfway through the cooking time, until the pasta is *al dente*.
— Drain the cooked pasta, dry by spreading on paper towel and set aside.
— Arrange a layer of lasagna in the bottom of the baking dish and cover with half the provolone and half the Gruyère cheese.
— Add a second layer of lasagna and cover with half the mozzarella and half the Parmesan cheese.
— Continue to layer the remaining pasta and cheese and sprinkle with the paprika.
— Cook at 70% for 9 to 11 minutes, giving the dish a half-turn halfway through the cooking time.

Lasagna with Salmon

Level of Difficulty	 🍴
Preparation Time	20 min
Cost per Serving	$
Number of Servings	8
Nutritional Value	304 calories 17.1 g protein 36.6 g carbohydrate
Food Exchanges	2 oz meat 2 bread exchanges 1/4 milk exchange
Cooking Time	40 min
Standing Time	None
Power Level	100%, 90%, 70%
Write Your Cooking Time Here	

Ingredients
225 g (8 oz) lasagna
225 g (8 oz) spinach lasagna
1 L (4 cups) water
5 mL (1 teaspoon) oil
10 mL (2 teaspoons) salt

Filling:
30 mL (2 tablespoons) butter
30 mL (2 tablespoons) flour
375 mL (1-1/2 cups) milk
salt and pepper to taste
30 mL (2 tablespoons) lemon juice
5 mL (1 teaspoon) Dijon mustard
225 g (8 oz) salmon, flaked
225 g (8 oz) smoked salmon, flaked
paprika to garnish

Method
— To cook the lasagna, pour the water into a rectangular dish and bring to the boil by heating at 100% for 8 to 10 minutes; add the oil, salt and the lasagna; cover and cook at 100% for 8 to 10 minutes, gently stirring several times to prevent sticking.
— Drain the cooked pasta, dry by spreading on a clean cloth and set aside.
— To prepare the filling, put the butter in a dish and heat at 100% for 45 seconds.
— Add the flour and mix well.
— Blend in the milk, beating with a wire whisk, and season to taste.
— Cook the sauce at 100% for 4 to 6 minutes, whisking every 2 minutes.
— Add the lemon juice and mustard to the sauce and mix well; heat at 90% for 1 to 2 minutes, stirring twice during the cooking time.
— Line the bottom of the

baking dish with a layer of lasagna; cover with half the sauce, half the flaked salmon and half the smoked salmon.
— Add another layer of lasagna and cover with the remaining sauce and salmon.
— If necessary, continue layering until all the ingredients are used.
— Sprinkle with paprika.
— Cook uncovered at 70% for 9 to 11 minutes and give the dish a half-turn halfway through the cooking time.

This recipe offers an original variation on classic lasagna. First assemble all the ingredients needed to prepare this unique dish.

Be Your Own Pasta Chef!

It seems that many people are under the impression that making pasta requires an in-depth knowledge of Italian cuisine or of food chemistry. Those without experience sometimes think that an imposing number of utensils are needed and therefore become discouraged before they even begin to discover the joys of pasta making. But once you realize that basic pasta dough is simply a combination of flour and water, the prospect of making your own pasta becomes less intimidating. In reality, it is not difficult to make pasta.

For your first experiments, the only equipment you really need includes a bowl, a spoon, a rolling pin and a knife. But most people soon find that they have developed a taste for pasta making and become more demanding in their utensil requirements. It is not long before the serious pasta maker acquires a pasta machine, a food processor, rollers, pastry cutters and molds—all allowing full rein to the imagination and helping in the production of fresh, savory pasta.

Homemade pasta is always a treat. Not only will you find it smoother in texture and more flavorful than dried pasta, but making it yourself allows you to vary your dishes to suit your own taste. Starting with a good pasta recipe it is certainly possible, even with very little equipment, to produce a tasty pasta which can be cut into strips to make fettuccine or lasagna. Even without molds, you can still cut and fill your own ravioli and tortellini. And with a special electric extrusion machine you can, without difficulty, produce an abundance of vermicelli and spaghetti.

The enthusiastic reactions created by your first attempts will no doubt encourage you to continue making other, more original kinds of pasta. Soon you will want to experiment not only with different shapes but also with different flavors. You will gain enough confidence to exchange your basic pasta recipe for more daring ones. Vegetables may begin to play a prominent role in your list of ingredients, and soon pasta made with tomatoes or spinach will appear on your table. Then you may well become intrigued with even more unusual variations, such as pasta made with pumpkin, beets or pistachios.

How to Make Fettuccine

Combine 500 mL (2 cups) flour and 5 mL (1 tsp) salt. Make a well in the center and add 3 beaten eggs and 30 to 45 mL (2 to 3 tbsp) olive oil. Using your hands, mix well, until the dough begins to stick together.

Turn the dough out onto a floured surface, knead until elastic (about 10 minutes), cover and set aside to rest for at least half an hour.

With a rolling pin, roll out the dough until it is as thin as possible.

Use the tip of a sharp knife to cut the dough into strips, without pulling it.

Repeat this operation, cutting the strips so that they are as uniform as possible.

Use the blade of the knife to lay the pasta strips on a lightly floured cloth before cooking.

The recipe above is a fairly basic pasta recipe. Whole wheat or buckwheat flour can also be used to make pasta, to be seasoned and garnished in different ways and served with different sauces.

For special occasions, or even for everyday meals, try preparing some brightly colored pasta for additional effect at the table. The use of beet purée will produce red pasta and, in the same way, the right amount of tomato sauce or tomato paste will give you a pink or orange color. Saffron will make your pasta yellow and spinach will add not only a green color but flavor as well. A mixture of delicate herbs will produce an interesting speckled effect. You will be able to produce so many variations in shape and color that your friends will be surprised when you remind them that the art of making pasta was originally one simple principle—the combining of flour and water.

Fettuccine with Red Wine

Ingredients
450 g (1 lb) fettuccine
1 L (4 cups) water
5 mL (1 teaspoon) salt
5 mL (1 teaspoon) oil

Sauce:
15 mL (1 tablespoon) oil
50 mL (1/4 cup) onion, finely chopped
1 garlic clove, crushed

200 g (7 oz) cooked bacon, crumbled
50 mL (1/4 cup) dry red wine
1 796 mL (28 oz) can of tomatoes, chopped
salt and pepper to taste
115 g (4 oz) Parmesan cheese, grated

Level of Difficulty	🍴
Preparation Time	15 min
Cost per Serving	**$**
Number of Servings	8
Nutritional Value	420 calories 18.6 g protein 39 g carbohydrate
Food Exchanges	2 oz meat 1 vegetable exchange 2 bread exchanges 2 fat exchanges
Cooking Time	32 min
Standing Time	None
Power Level	100%
Write Your Cooking Time Here	

Method
— To make the sauce, put the oil into a dish, add the onion and garlic, and cook at 100% for 3 minutes, stirring once.
— Add the bacon and wine and cook at 100% for 3 minutes, stirring once.
— Add the tomatoes and season to taste; continue to cook at 100% for 7 to 10 minutes, stirring twice; set aside.
— To cook the pasta, bring the water to the boil by heating at 100% for 8 to 10 minutes.
— Add the salt, oil and the fettuccine and cook at 100% for 5 to 7 minutes, stirring twice.
— Drain the fettuccine, reheat the sauce, and pour it over the pasta.
— Garnish with the Parmesan cheese.

Fettuccine with Roquefort Cheese

Level of Difficulty	🍴🍴
Preparation Time	1 h 30 min
Cost per Serving	$
Number of Servings	5
Nutritional Value	285 calories 11.2 g protein 31.5 g carbohydrates
Food Exchanges	1 oz meat 2 bread exchanges 1 fat exchange
Cooking Time	18 min
Standing Time	None
Power Level	100%, 70%
Write Your Cooking Time Here	

Ingredients
Fettuccine:
3 eggs
500 mL (2 cups) unbleached all purpose flour
5 mL (1 teaspoon) salt
1 L (4 cups) water, for cooking
5 mL (1 teaspoon) salt, for cooking
5 mL (1 teaspoon) oil, for cooking

Sauce:
125 mL (1/2 cup) Roquefort cheese
75 mL (5 tablespoons) 35% cream
pepper to taste

Method
— To make the pasta dough, beat the eggs lightly, without frothing.
— Put the flour and salt in a large bowl, make a small well in the center and pour in the beaten eggs.
— Combine the flour and the eggs, mixing until the pasta is firm.
— Knead the dough until it is elastic and let rest for 30 minutes.
— Divide the pasta dough into three equal portions.
— Using a rolling pin, roll out each portion of dough until it is as thin as possible.
— Let the thin sheets of dough dry for 10 minutes, until they lose their stickiness.
— Roll each sheet of pasta into a long, cylindrical jelly-roll shape.
— With a sharp knife, cut the tube of pasta into thin slices.
— Unroll the sliced pasta strips and lay them, spread out, on a lightly floured cloth.
— Let rest for another 10 minutes to firm up slightly.
— To cook the pasta, pour

the water into a dish and bring to the boil by heating at 100% for 8 to 10 minutes; add the salt, oil and the fettuccine and cook at 100% for 4 to 5 minutes, stirring twice to avoid sticking.
— In the meantime, prepare the sauce. Break up the Roquefort cheese with a fork, add the cream and the pepper and mix well.
— Drain the cooked pasta and pour into a dish.
— Pour the Roquefort and cream mixture over the fettuccine and coat well.

— Reduce the power to 70% and heat for 2 to 3 minutes, stirring once.

This recipe is easy to make and brings out the special texture of homemade fettuccine. First assemble all the ingredients required.

Pasta Filled with a Surprise

Of all the different kinds of pasta, the filled pastas are probably the most satisfying and the most enjoyable to make at home. Because so many different fillings are possible for them, they can be quite fascinating—each a surprise until the first bite is taken. It might be said that filled pasta constitutes the "cream" of the pasta families.

There are two main types of filled pasta: closed and open. Ravioli is the most familiar of the closed category, which also includes agnolotti (half-circles with scalloped edges) and round ravioli (also called medallions). Open pasta includes, in the main, manicotti (large, grooved cannelloni), cannelloni and large and small shells.

The delights of filled pasta served with sauce are well known, but this pasta group is also delicious simmered in flavorful soups or as an ingredient in salads, particularly in bean salad. Some very daring chefs are even suggesting sweetening ravioli for desserts—a praline ravioli, for example.

The number of recipes for fillings is practically infinite and new discoveries are being made every day. Ground meat fillings are well known; a particularly delicious filling combines ground beef and spinach with white wine, generously seasoned with fresh thyme.

Cheese-based fillings are also frequently used and some of these may include mashed potatoes. Pasta filled with goat cheese, accented with a touch of lemon juice, makes a refreshing change in salads. Seafood, another ingredient found in pasta fillings, inspires any number of combinations: fish, shrimp butter and cream; scallops and potatoes; sardines and so on. For special occasions lobster meat, seasoned with green onions, chives, mushrooms, cream and wine or cognac, makes a memorable filling.

As you can see, the possibilities for pasta fillings are endless and impressive. They invite you to explore new options and astonish your guests.

Cannelloni with Veal and Spinach

Level of Difficulty	🍴🍴
Preparation Time	20 min
Cost per Serving	$
Number of Servings	6
Nutritional Value	334 calories 25.3 g protein 27.6 g carbohydrate
Food Exchanges	3 oz meat 2 vegetable exchanges 1 bread exchange
Cooking Time	40 min
Standing Time	None
Power Level	100%, 70%
Write Your Cooking Time Here	

Ingredients
12 cannelloni
1 L (4 cups) water
5 mL (1 teaspoon) salt
5 mL (1 teaspoon) oil
250 mL (1 cup) tomato sauce

Filling:
1 onion, finely chopped
1 clove garlic, crushed
450 g (1 lb) ground veal
450 g (1 lb) spinach, chopped
1 egg
60 mL (4 tablespoons)
breadcrumbs
50 mL (1/4 cup) Parmesan
cheese, grated

Method
— To prepare the filling, put the onion and garlic in a dish and cook at 100% for 2 to 3 minutes.
— Add the veal and cook at 100% for 6 to 7 minutes, stirring and breaking up the meat with a spoon every 3 minutes.
— Add the spinach and continue to cook at 100% for 2 to 3 minutes.
— Add the egg, breadcrumbs and Parmesan to the cooked meat mixture, stir well to ensure a uniform consistency and set aside.
— To cook the cannelloni, pour the water into a dish and bring to the boil by heating at 100% for 6 to 9 minutes; add the salt, oil and the cannelloni and cook at 100% for 7 to 8 minutes, stirring twice during the cooking time.
— Drain the cannelloni and stuff with the prepared filling.
— Put the cannelloni into a dish and cover with the tomato sauce.
— Reduce the power to 70% and cook for 8 to 10 minutes.
— Sprinkle with Parmesan cheese before serving.

Stir with a spoon every 3 minutes to break up the pieces of ground veal.

Add the egg, breadcrumbs and Parmesan to the meat mixture and mix well to obtain a uniform consistency.

Drain the cooked cannelloni and stuff with the prepared filling.

How To Make Ravioli

Prepare the pasta dough (see page 58) and form into a smooth ball; place in a bowl, cover and refrigerate for 2 hours.

Remove the pasta dough from the refrigerator and divide it into two equal parts. Roll the dough out, until it is as thin as possible, to obtain two sheets of the same size.

Place teaspoonfuls (5 mL each) of the filling in rows with an equal distance, about 5 cm (2 in), between them on one of the sheets.

Using a pastry brush, moisten the dough between the pockets of filling with water, laying the other sheet of pasta dough on top.

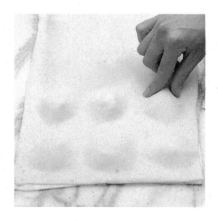

Press around the pockets of filling with your fingers so that the two sheets of pasta dough stick together and are well sealed.

With a pastry wheel, cut squares around the pockets of filling to make the ravioli.

Spinach and Veal Filling

Ingredients
225 g (8 oz) ground veal
225 g (8 oz) ham, chopped
450 g (1 lb) spinach
30 mL (2 tablespoons) butter
1 onion, minced
125 mL (1/2 cup) white wine
2 egg yolks
salt and pepper to taste

Method
— Put the spinach in a dish and cook covered at 100% for 4 to 5 minutes, stirring once.
— Drain the spinach, chop finely and set aside.
— In a casserole melt the butter and add the onion, veal, ham and wine; cook at 100% for 7 to 8 minutes, occasionally breaking up the meat with a fork.
— Add the cooked spinach and egg yolks, season to taste, and mix all the ingredients well.

Manicotti with Pike

Ingredients
12 manicotti
1 L (4 cups) water
5 mL (1 teaspoon) salt
5 mL (1 teaspoon) oil

Filling:
450 g (1 lb) fillet of pike
1 bay leaf
75 mL (1/3 cup) 35% cream
salt and pepper to taste

Sauce:
50 mL (1/4 cup) butter
50 mL (1/4 cup) flour
500 mL (2 cups) milk
salt and pepper to taste
125 mL (1/2 cup) Parmesan
cheese, grated
30 mL (2 tablespoons)
parsley, chopped
paprika to garnish

Method
— To cook the manicotti, pour the water into a rectangular dish and bring to the boil by heating at 100% for 8 to 10 minutes; add the salt, oil and the pasta. Cook at 100% for 7 to 9 minutes, giving the dish a half-turn halfway through the cooking time.
— Drain the cooked pasta, rinse in cold water, and let dry on a clean cloth.
— To prepare the filling, put the pike fillets and the bay leaf in a dish; cover and cook at 90% for 5 to 6 minutes, giving the dish a half-turn after 3 minutes.
— Drain the cooking liquid produced, discard the bay leaf, and flake the fillets of pike with a fork.
— Add the cream to the fish and season to taste.
— Fill the manicotti with the mixture.
— To prepare the sauce, put the butter in a dish and heat at 100% for 1 minute to melt.
— Add the flour and mix well; blend in the milk and cook at 100% for 5 to 7 minutes, stirring every 2 minutes.
— Season to taste and add the parsley and 50 mL (1/4 cup) of the Parmesan.
— Put the filled manicotti into a dish, pour the sauce over it, and sprinkle with the remaining Parmesan and the paprika.
— Heat at 50% for 5 to 6 minutes, giving the dish a half-turn halfway through the cooking time.

Tortellini with Cream

Level of Difficulty	▯▯▯ ▯▯▯
Preparation Time	1 h 30 min
Cost per Serving	**$**
Number of Servings	8
Nutritional Value	426 calories 15 g protein 24 g carbohydrate
Food Exchanges	2 oz meat 1-1/2 bread exchanges 3-1/2 fat exchanges
Cooking Time	24 min
Standing Time	None
Power Level	100%, 70%
Write Your Cooking Time Here	

Ingredients
Tortellini:
3 eggs
500 mL (2 cups) unbleached all purpose flour
5 mL (1 teaspoon) salt
1 L (4 cups) water, for cooking
5 mL (1 teaspoon) salt, for cooking
5 mL (1 teaspoon) oil, for cooking

Filling:
250 mL (1 cup) spinach
250 mL (1 cup) ricotta cheese
125 mL (1/2 cup) Parmesan cheese, grated
2 eggs, beaten
salt and pepper to taste

Sauce:
500 mL (2 cups) 35% cream
30 mL (2 tablespoons) melted butter
15 mL (1 tablespoon) Parmesan cheese, grated

Method
— To prepare the pasta, beat the eggs slightly, without frothing.
— Combine the flour and salt in a large bowl, make a small well in the center, and pour in the eggs.
— Mix the flour and the eggs to obtain a firm consistency.
— Knead the dough until elastic and let rest for 30 minutes.
— In the meantime, cook the spinach in a covered dish at 100% for 4 to 5 minutes, stirring once during the cooking time; remove the spinach, drain carefully, and chop finely.
— Prepare the filling by combining the spinach, ricotta, Parmesan, eggs and seasoning; mix well and set aside.
— Divide the dough into two equal portions.
— Roll out the dough with a rolling pin until as thin as possible.
— Use a 6 cm (2-1/2 in) cookie cutter to cut rounds of dough.
— Place a small mound of filling on each round, fold the dough over the filling and, using your fingers, press the edges together.
— Pinch the two ends together to form a circle.
— To cook the pasta, pour the water into a dish and bring to the boil by heating at 100% for 8 to 10 minutes; add the salt, oil and the tortellini and cook at 100% for 4 to 5 minutes.
— Drain the cooked tortellini and set aside.
— To prepare the sauce, combine the cream, melted butter and Parmesan cheese in a dish and mix well; reduce the power to 70% and cook for 3 to 4 minutes, stirring twice during the cooking time.
— Pour the sauce over the tortellini and serve immediately.

Ravioli in Soup

Level of Difficulty	
Preparation Time	5 min
Cost per Serving	**$**
Number of Servings	4
Nutritional Value	366 calories 15.2 g protein 34 g carbohydrate
Food Exchanges	2 oz meat 2 bread exchanges 1-1/2 fat exchanges
Cooking Time	18 min
Standing Time	None
Power Level	100%, 70%
Write Your Cooking Time Here	

Ingredients
450 g (1 lb) meat-filled ravioli
1 L (4 cups) beef broth
125 mL (1/2 cup) sour cream
75 mL (1/3 cup) Madeira wine
2 egg yolks, beaten
salt and pepper to taste
15 mL (1 tablespoon) parsley, chopped

Method
— Pour the beef broth into a dish and heat at 100% for 7 to 8 minutes or until boiling.
— Add the ravioli and cook at 100% for 4 to 5 minutes, stirring once during the cooking time.
— Pour the sour cream into a bowl, add the Madeira and the beaten egg yolks and mix well.
— Add the sour cream mixture to the broth and ravioli, season with salt and pepper, reduce the power to 70% and heat for 4 to 5 minutes.
— Garnish with parsley before serving.

Assemble all the ingredients required to prepare this magnificent soup.

Add the ravioli to the hot beef broth and cook at 100% for 4 to 5 minutes, stirring once.

In a bowl combine the sour cream, Madeira wine and beaten egg yolks and add to the broth.

MICROTIPS

Pasta with a Splendid Yellow Color

Adding a small amount of saffron to the ingredients used to make pasta will give your homemade dough a lively yellow color.

Ravioli with Scallops and Fennel

Level of Difficulty	🍴🍴 🍴
Preparation Time	1 h*
Cost per Serving	$ $
Number of Servings	10
Nutritional Value	429 calories 26.2 g protein 1.7 g carbohydrate
Food Exchanges	2 oz meat 2-1/2 bread exchanges 1-1/2 fat exchanges
Cooking Time	29 min
Standing Time	None
Power Level	100%, 70%
Write Your Cooking Time Here	

* The dough should be refrigerated for 2 hours before using it.

Ingredients

Ravioli:
1 L (4 cups) unbleached all purpose flour
5 eggs, beaten
15 mL (1 tablespoon) vinegar
30 mL (2 tablespoons) lard, melted
pinch salt
1 L (4 cups) water, for cooking
5 mL (1 teaspoon) salt, for cooking
5 mL (1 teaspoon) oil, for cooking

Filling:
900 g (2 lb) scallops
450 g (1 lb) fennel, chopped
2 green onions, chopped
50 mL (1/4 cup) butter
2 egg yolks
30 mL (2 tablespoons) 35% cream
250 mL (1 cup) white wine

30 mL (2 tablespoons)
liquorice-based aperitif
(Pernod or Ricard)

Sauce:
2 green onions, chopped
75 mL (1/3 cup) white wine
150 mL (2/3 cup) 35% cream
15 mL (1 tablespoon) lemon
juice

Method
— To make the ravioli
dough, combine all the
ingredients required for
the pasta in a bowl and
mix well.
— Using the heel of your
hand, knead the dough
until it forms a smooth
ball.
— Put the dough into a
covered dish and
refrigerate for 2 hours.
— In the meantime, prepare
the filling by first
combining the fennel,
green onions and butter;
cook at 100% for 5 to 6
minutes and set aside.
— Dice the scallops.
— Beat the egg yolks and add
the cream, white wine and
aperitif; add the scallops
and mix well.
— Blend this mixture with the
fennel, green onion and
butter and stir until
smooth.
— Cook at 70% for 1 to 2
minutes.
— Drain the filling through a
sieve, retaining the liquid.
— Set aside both the liquid
and the filling.
— Remove the dough from
the refrigerator after 2
hours and divide it into
two; roll each portion out
with a rolling pin to
obtain two sheets of
dough, equal in size and
as thin as possible.
— Spoon a small amount (5
mL or 1 teaspoon) of the
prepared filling onto one
of the sheets of dough at
equal distances, about 5
cm (2 in) apart.
— With a pastry brush,
moisten the dough
between the mounds of
filling with water and
cover with the other sheet.
— With your fingers, press
down on the dough
around the pockets of
filling so that the two
sheets of pasta stick
together.
— Use a pastry cutter to cut
squares around the
pockets of filling to make
the ravioli.
— To cook the ravioli, pour ⟹

Ravioli with Scallops and Fennel

the water into a large dish and bring to the boil by heating at 100% for 8 to 10 minutes; add the salt, oil and the ravioli and cook at 100% for 4 to 5 minutes, stirring twice during the cooking time; set the cooked ravioli aside.

— To prepare the sauce, combine the green onions and the white wine in a dish and cook at 100% for 2 to 3 minutes, stirring once during the cooking time.
— Add the cooking liquid from the scallops and cook at 100% for 2 to 3

minutes, stirring once during the cooking time.
— Add the cream and lemon juice and mix well.
— Pour the sauce over the cooked ravioli and serve immediately.

MICROTIPS

Keeping Grated Cheese on Hand

Most people do not particularly enjoy cleaning utensils, especially when it comes to cheese graters. Unfortunately, if you want to enjoy freshly grated cheese there is no way around it; you must use a grater. To reduce the time spent scouring, you can prepare large amounts of grated cheese at one time and set unneeded portions aside for later use.

First, buy a large quantity of cheese—take advantage of a sale. Grate all the cheese and divide it into freezer bags so that each bag contains enough cheese for one

recipe. Seal the bags carefully and freeze.

Cheese that is grated defrosts quickly at room temperature. If the bag is well sealed, the cheese won't dry out and will keep for several weeks in the freezer without losing its freshness or its flavor.

To Cook Cannelloni and Lasagna Quickly

If not too thick, cannelloni and lasagna noodles can be cooked at the same time as their filling and sauce. First, however, make sure that the sauce is fairly liquid and that it completely covers the cannelloni or lasagna noodles. To save time, layer the lasagna or fill the cannelloni in the same way that you would if it had been cooked,

but add 25% more sauce and cook for the same amount of time. This tip is a valuable time saver.

Using a Variety of Cheeses

The creamy texture of mozzarella and the lively taste of Parmesan are both delicious and it can be difficult to decide which cheese to use when preparing a dish of pasta. Therefore, why choose at all? Why not combine your favorite cheeses and enjoy them together? Parmesan goes very well with both ricotta and cottage cheese, and Gruyère and mozzarella make another favorite combination. But, in fact, the best combinations are probably the ones you choose yourself.

Macaroni with Cheddar Cheese

Ingredients
375 mL (1-1/2 cups) macaroni
1.5 L (6 cups) water
5 mL (1 teaspoon) oil
5 mL (1 teaspoon) salt

125 mL (1/2 cup)
mushrooms, cooked
125 mL (1/2 cup) onions,
cooked
250 mL (1 cup) broccoli,

cooked
284 mL (10 oz) can of cream
of mushroom soup
125 mL (1/2 cup) milk
500 mL (2 cups) orange
cheddar cheese, grated

Level of Difficulty	🍴
Preparation Time	10 min
Cost per Serving	**$**
Number of Servings	6
Nutritional Value	310 calories 14.5 g protein 24 g carbohydrate
Food Exchanges	1-1/2 oz meat 2 vegetable exchanges 1 fat exchange 1 bread exchange 1/4 milk exchange
Cooking Time	19 min
Standing Time	None
Power Level	100%, 70%
Write Your Cooking Time Here	✏️

Method
— Bring the water to the boil, add the oil, salt and macaroni; cook at 100% for 7 to 9 minutes, stirring twice during the cooking time. Drain and set aside.
— Put the cooked vegetables in a dish, cover and heat at 100% for 2 to 3 minutes.
— Pour the cream of mushroom soup into a bowl, add the milk and the cheddar cheese and mix well; cook at 100% for 4 to 5 minutes, stirring every 2 minutes.
— Add the macaroni and the cooked vegetables to the sauce, heat at 70% for 2 minutes and serve.

Linguine with Mushrooms and Cream

Level of Difficulty	(icon)
Preparation Time	15 min
Cost per Serving	$
Number of Servings	8
Nutritional Value	466 calories 17 g protein 37.2 g carbohydrate
Food Exchanges	2 oz meat 1 vegetable exchange 2 bread exchanges 3 fat exchanges
Cooking Time	15 min
Standing Time	None
Power Level	100%
Write Your Cooking Time Here	(icon)

Ingredients
450 g (1 lb) linguine, cooked
8 slices of bacon
225 g (8 oz) mushrooms, sliced
1 onion, sliced
500 mL (2 cups) 35% cream
500 mL (2 cups) mozzarella cheese, grated
salt and pepper to taste
garlic powder to taste

Method
— Put the bacon slices on a rack and cook at 100% for 6 to 8 minutes; crumble and set aside.
— Cook the mushrooms and onions in a dish at 100% for 2 to 3 minutes; drain and set aside.
— Pour the cream into a bowl and heat at 100% for 2 to 3 minutes, add the mozzarella cheese and beat with a whisk to mix well; continue to cook at 100% for 1 minute and stir.
— Add the cooked vegetables and the pasta to the sauce and season to taste.
— Add the crumbled bacon and mix well.
— Reheat if necessary and serve immediately.

These flavorful ingredients combine to create this delicious linguine dish.

Crumble the cooked bacon and set aside.

Add the grated mozzarella to the hot cream and beat with a whisk to blend.

Gnocchi with Cream

Level of Difficulty	
Preparation Time	30 min
Cost per Serving	$
Number of Servings	8
Nutritional Value	328 calories 8.3 g protein 30.8 g carbohydrate
Food Exchanges	1 vegetable exchange 2 bread exchanges 3 fat exchanges
Cooking Time	31 min + cooking time for dumplings
Standing Time	None
Power Level	100%, 70%
Write Your Cooking Time Here	

Ingredients
Pasta:
900 g (2 lb) potatoes, peeled
125 mL (1/2 cup) water
45 mL (3 tablespoons) butter
2 eggs
2 egg yolks
250 mL (1 cup) flour
pinch nutmeg
salt and pepper to taste
750 mL (3 cups) water, to cook the pasta

Sauce:
15 mL (1 tablespoon) butter
2 green onions, chopped
125 mL (1/2 cup) Italian-style tomatoes, chopped
10 mL (2 teaspoons) fine herbs
2 mL (1/2 teaspoon) oregano
2 mL (1/2 teaspoon) basil
250 mL (1 cup) 35% cream
75 mL (1/3 cup) Parmesan cheese, grated

Method
— To prepare the gnocchi, place the potatoes into a dish and add 125 mL (1/2 cup) water; cover and cook at 100% for 6 to 8 minutes, stirring twice during the cooking time.
— Drain the cooked potatoes and reserve the cooking liquid.
— Use an electric hand beater to purée the potatoes while adding the butter, eggs, egg yolks, flour, nutmeg, salt and pepper; set aside.
— To cook the gnocchi, pour the water used for cooking the potatoes dish and add 750 mL (3 cups) of water; bring to the boil by heating at 100% for 9 to 10 minutes.
— Drop small spoonfuls of the dough into the boiling water and remove them with a slotted spoon as they come to the surface; continue this operation until all the dough is used and set the cooked gnocchi aside.
— To prepare the sauce, put the butter into a dish and melt at 100% for 30 seconds; add the green onions and cook at 100% for 2 minutes, stirring

once during the cooking time.
— Add the tomatoes and the seasoning and cook at 100% for 3 minutes.
— Add the cream and mix well; cook at 70% for 2 to 3 minutes.

— Blend in the Parmesan cheese, stirring to obtain a smooth consistency.
— Add the gnocchi to the sauce and reheat at 70% for 3 to 5 minutes or until the dish is hot.

Gnocchi with cream is a favorite dish of pasta lovers. First assemble the ingredients needed for this recipe.

Rice—An Underrated Staple

Rice is both a grain and a cereal; the plant that produces it also produces coarse stalks of cereal grass. This farinaceous grain feeds one third of the world's population, making rice and wheat the most highly consumed foods in the world.

While we in the West consider rice to be a side dish, like bread or potatoes, in the Orient it is the basis of all food consumed there. The fact is that we are familiar with only some of the standard varieties of the 7000 different kinds of rice known in the East, all of which, with the exception of wild rice, belong to the same family. We are familiar with rice as it grows naturally in water or is cultivated in rice paddies, but we know very little about mountain rices that grow in tropical climates, requiring very little water. Lovers of oriental rice can distinguish, by taste and appearance, long grain rice from short grain rice and pointed grain rice from flattened rice. Other varieties they appreciate include white rice speckled with black, ivory rice, purple rice, and some naturally fragrant rices. But,

unfortunately, to most of us in the West rice is just rice.

Of course, our lack of knowledge is probably due to the fact that the West does not have a long tradition of rice consumption. In China rice has been a staple food for over 5000 years but, in spite of this long history, the Chinese are not the pioneers in the cultivation of rice. This distinction belongs to India, where a wild grass called "newaree" was first grown. This grass is the ancestor of the rice we know today, *Oryza sativa*. Centuries of rice cultivation have altered this plant and have produced the many varieties now available.

Some of the rice we consume is produced in North America. On this continent rice was first cultivated in North Carolina and was so successful that it was called the "gold of Carolina."

Many different types of rice are now available: the most common are long grain, medium grain and short grain rice; white and brown rice; semi-cooked and instant rice; and basmati rice, an Indian rice with a very distinct flavor.

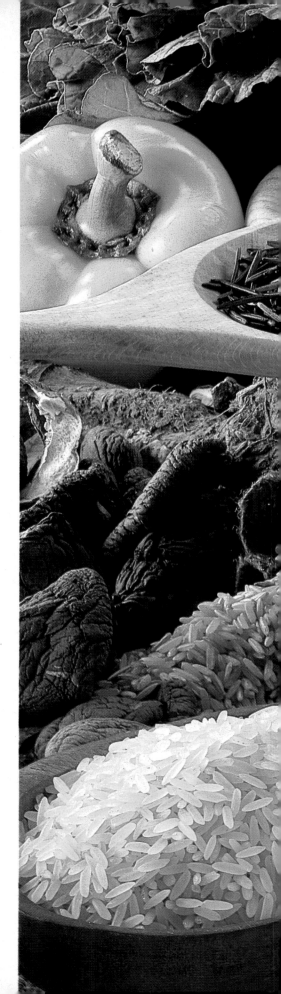

Rice Pilaf

Level of Difficulty	🍴
Preparation Time	10 min
Cost per Serving	$
Number of Servings	4
Nutritional Value	150 calories 8.8 g protein 20 g carbohydrate
Food Exchanges	1/2 vegetable exchange 1 bread exchange 1 fat exchange
Cooking Time	19 min
Standing Time	10 min
Power Level	100%, 70%
Write Your Cooking Time Here	

Ingredients
250 mL (1 cup) long grain rice
30 mL (2 tablespoons) butter
2 chicken bouillon cubes
425 mL (1-3/4 cups) boiling water
45 mL (3 tablespoons) celery, diced
45 mL (3 tablespoons) green onions, sliced
30 mL (2 tablespoons) soy sauce
75 mL (1/3 cup) mushrooms, sliced

Method
— Put the butter in a casserole and melt at 100% for 30 seconds; add the rice and brown at 100% for 3 to 4 minutes and then stir once.
— Dissolve the chicken bouillon cubes in the boiling water and add the liquid to the rice.
— Add the celery, green onions and soy sauce and mix well.
— Cover and cook at 100% for 5 minutes.
— Reduce the power to 70% and continue to cook for 10 minutes.
— Add the mushrooms and stir with a fork.
— Cover and let stand for 10 minutes before serving.

Assemble the ingredients needed for this delicious classic recipe.

Add the rice to the melted butter and cook at 100% for 3 to 4 minutes until brown and then stir once.

MICROTIPS

Cooking Times for Rice

Cooking times vary according to the type of rice used.
Brown rice: 30 minutes
Long grain white rice: 15 minutes
Precooked rice: 5 minutes

Fried Rice with Shrimp

Level of Difficulty	🍴
Preparation Time	10 min
Cost per Serving	$ $
Number of Servings	2
Nutritional Value	586 calories 18.8 g protein 62.3 g carbohydrate
Food Exchanges	2 oz meat 3 bread exchanges 4 fat exchanges
Cooking Time	24 min
Standing Time	None
Power Level	100%, 70%
Write Your Cooking Time Here	

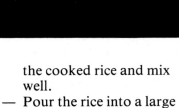

Ingredients
250 mL (1 cup) long grain rice
500 mL (2 cups) boiling water
250 mL (1 cup) shrimp
50 mL (1/4 cup) oil
45 mL (3 tablespoons) soy sauce
60 mL (4 tablespoons) brown sugar
5 mL (1 teaspoon) salt

Method
— Pour the boiling water into a casserole, add the rice; cover and cook at 100% for 5 minutes.
— Reduce the power to 70% and continue to cook for 10 minutes.
— In the meantime, combine the oil, soy sauce, brown sugar and salt and beat with a whisk until smooth.
— Add this combination to the cooked rice and mix well.
— Pour the rice into a large dish and distribute evenly.
— Cook uncovered at 100% for 4 to 6 minutes, stirring after 2 minutes.
— Add the shrimp, continue to cook at 100% for 2 to 3 minutes, and stir once.

To cook rice in the microwave oven, simply place it in a casserole with hot water.

Beat the mixture of oil, soy sauce, brown sugar and salt with a whisk until smooth.

Add the shrimp to the rice before the final stage of cooking.

Wild Rice

Level of Difficulty	🍴🍽
Preparation Time	25 min
Cost per Serving	$ $
Number of Servings	4
Nutritional Value	431 calories 25 g protein 40 g carbohydrate
Food Exchanges	2-1/2 oz meat 2 bread exchanges 2 fat exchanges
Cooking Time	41 min
Standing Time	None
Power Level	100%, 90%, 70%
Write Your Cooking Time Here	

Ingredients
250 mL (1 cup) wild rice
30 mL (2 tablespoons) butter
375 mL (1-1/2 cups) chicken, cut into strips
625 mL (2-1/2 cups) boiling water
250 mL (1 cup) broccoli
45 mL (3 tablespoons) water
125 mL (1/2 cup) sour cream

Method
— Preheat a browning dish at 100% for 7 minutes; add the butter and heat at 100% for 30 seconds.
— Sear the chicken, cover and cook at 90% for 3 to 4 minutes or until cooked, stirring once during the cooking time; set aside.
— Pour the boiling water into a dish and add the wild rice; cover and cook at 100% for 5 minutes.
— Reduce the power to 70% and cook for 20 to 25 minutes, giving the dish a half-turn after 10 minues; set aside.
— Pour the 45 mL (3 tablespoons) of water into a dish and add the broccoli; cover and cook at 100% for 3 to 4 minutes, stirring once after 2 minutes.
— In a large casserole, combine the chicken, broccoli and rice; add the sour cream and mix well.
— Cook at 70% for 2 to 3 minutes or until heated through.

Sear the strips of chicken in butter in a preheated browning dish.

Cook the broccoli in a covered dish, stirring once after 2 minutes.

MICROTIPS

Use Leftover Rice in Soups

When you have rice left over, but not quite enough to make another meal, simply use it in your homemade soups. Add the rice just before the soup is completely cooked.

Rice Quiche

Level of Difficulty	(difficulty icon)
Preparation Time	20 min
Cost per Serving	$
Number of Servings	6
Nutritional Value	343 calories 18.2 g protein 15.4 g carbohydrate
Food Exchanges	2 oz meat 1 vegetable exchange 1 bread exchange 2 fat exchanges
Cooking Time	42 min
Standing Time	4 min
Power Level	100%, 70%
Write Your Cooking Time Here	

Ingredients
175 mL (3/4 cup) long grain rice
500 mL (2 cups) boiling water
15 mL (1 tablespoon) butter
8 slices of bacon
1 onion, chopped
115 g (4 oz) mushrooms, sliced
1 green pepper, chopped
1 tomato, chopped
salt and pepper to taste
4 eggs
250 mL (1 cup) 18% cream
15 mL (1 tablespoon) flour
375 mL (1-1/2 cups) mozzarella cheese, grated
paprika to garnish

Method
— Grease the inside of a quiche mold with the butter.
— Pour the boiling water into a dish and add the rice; cook at 100% for 5 minutes.
— Reduce the power to 70%, cook for 10 minutes longer, and let cool.
— Line the bottom of the quiche mold with the rice and set aside.
— Place the slices of bacon in a dish and cook at 100% for 8 to 10 minutes, until crispy.
— Remove the bacon from the dish, retaining the bacon fat.
— Add the onion, mushrooms and green pepper to the bacon fat and cook at 100% for 2 to 3 minutes.
— Crumble the bacon and add to the cooked vegetables.
— Add the chopped tomato, season to taste, and mix well.
— Spread the mixture over the rice in the quiche mold and set aside.
— In a bowl, beat the eggs and add the cream, flour and a little salt; beat until smooth and creamy.
— Pour this mixture over the vegetables and bacon.
— Top with the grated cheese and sprinkle with paprika.
— Place the quiche mold on a raised rack in the oven and cook at 70% for 12 to 14 minutes, giving the dish a half-turn halfway through the cooking time.
— Let stand for 4 minutes before serving.

Rice with Pork and Vegetables

Level of Difficulty	🍴
Preparation Time	25 min
Cost per Serving	$ $
Number of Servings	4
Nutritional Value	464 calories 29.2 g protein 42.5 g carbohydrate
Food Exchanges	3 oz meat 2 vegetable exchanges 2 bread exchanges 1 fat exchange
Cooking Time	24 min
Standing Time	None
Power Level	100%, 70%
Write Your Cooking Time Here	

Ingredients
500 mL (2 cups) long grain rice
1 L (4 cups) boiling water
30 mL (2 tablespoons) butter
450 g (1 lb) pork cutlets, cut into strips
2 cloves garlic, crushed
1 red pepper, thinly sliced
1 green pepper, thinly sliced
500 mL (2 cups) tomatoes, peeled and chopped
30 mL (2 tablespoons) parsley, chopped
salt and pepper to taste

Method
— Preheat a browning dish at 100% for 7 minutes; add the butter and heat at 100% for 30 seconds.
— Sear the pork in the dish and add the garlic.
— Add the peppers and cook covered at 100% for 3 to 4 minutes.
— Add the tomatoes, parsley, boiling water and rice and cook at 100% for 5 minutes.
— Stir and continue to cook at 70% for 13 to 15 minutes, until the rice is cooked.
— Season to taste before serving.

These are the ingredients needed to prepare this recipe, one that is suitable for any occasion.

After searing the pork in the browning dish, add the peppers and cook as directed in the recipe.

MICROTIPS

Freezing and Defrosting Leftover Rice

It is quite often that we cook too much rice for one meal, but this tendency is no problem with a microwave oven. Leftover rice can be frozen and defrosted in the microwave, and it will retain all its nutritional value as well as its flavor.

Divide the leftover rice into 250 mL (1 cup) or 500 mL (2 cup) quantities and place in freezer bags. Date the bags, seal them well, and freeze. The rice will keep for up to 6 months. To defrost a package, pour the contents into a dish that is twice the volume of the rice and place in the microwave oven at 70%. It takes 2 to 3 minutes to defrost a 125 mL (1/2 cup) serving and 4 to 8 minutes to defrost a 250 mL (1 cup) serving. Stir once during the defrosting process.

Rice and Vegetable Stuffing

Level of Difficulty	
Preparation Time	10 min*
Cost per Serving	$
Number of Servings	2
Nutritional Value	170 calories 6.6 g protein 23 g carbohydrate
Food Exchanges	4 vegetable exchanges 1/2 bread exchange 1/4 milk exchange 1/2 fat exchange
Cooking Time	6 min
Standing Time	None
Power Level	100%
Write Your Cooking Time Here	

* The stuffing must be allowed to cool before serving.

Ingredients
125 mL (1/2 cup) brown rice, cooked
125 mL (1/2 cup) onion, finely chopped
125 mL (1/2 cup) celery, diced
125 mL (1/2 cup) carrots, grated
50 mL (1/4 cup) water
30 mL (2 tablespoons) walnuts, chopped
125 mL (1/2 cup) plain yoghurt

Method
— Put the onions, celery and carrots in a dish and add the water; cover and cook at 100% for 5 to 6 minutes, stirring once during the cooking time.
— Drain the vegetables, add the cooked rice and the chopped walnuts and mix well.
— Add the yoghurt and allow the stuffing to cool before using.

These few ingredients are all you need to make this tasty stuffing.

MICROTIPS

For Fluffy Rice

When using rice as an ingredient in salads, it is important that the grains of rice separate easily and do not stick together. To obtain this consistency, two rules should be followed.

First, choose a long grain rice. Whether using brown, white or semi-cooked rice, long grain rice does not stick together as easily as short grain rice. Therefore, use only long grain rice for salads.

The second rule involves the way in which the rice is cooked. Do not stir the rice as it cooks—the less the rice is stirred, the less starch is released and, therefore, the rice is not as likely to stick together.

Rice and Orange Stuffing

Level of Difficulty	🍴
Preparation Time	15 min
Cost per Serving	**$**
Number of Servings	4
Nutritional Value	184 calories 3.3 g protein 30 g carbohydrate
Food Exchanges	1 vegetable exchange 1/2 fruit exchange 1 bread exchange 1 fat exchange
Cooking Time	15 min
Standing Time	10 min
Power Level	100%, 70%
Write Your Cooking Time Here	

Ingredients
250 mL (1 cup) long grain rice
250 mL (1 cup) hot chicken stock
250 mL (1 cup) hot orange juice
15 mL (1 tablespoon) orange zest, grated
50 mL (1/4 cup) celery, finely chopped
50 mL (1/4 cup) onion, finely chopped
30 mL (2 tablespoons) butter
150 mL (2/3 cup) oranges, diced
15 mL (1 tablespoon) parsley, chopped

Method
— In a casserole, combine all the ingredients except the diced orange and the parsley.
— Cover and cook at 100% for 5 minutes.
— Stir the mixture, cover again, reduce the power to 70% and continue to cook for 10 minutes.
— Add the diced orange and sprinkle with the parsley.
— Let stand for 10 minutes before serving.

This delicious stuffing will be an instant favorite. First assemble the required ingredients.

MICROTIPS

Making Croquettes or Rice Pudding

Choose short grain or medium grain rice when making croquettes or rice pudding. These types of rice stick together more than will long grain rice.

Combine all the ingredients except the diced orange and the parsley in a casserole and cook as directed in the recipe.

Add the diced orange, sprinkle with parsley and let stand for 10 minutes.

Lemon Rice

Ingredients
250 mL (1 cup) long grain rice
375 mL (1-1/2 cups) boiling
water

125 mL (1/2 cup) lemon juice
30 mL (2 tablespoons)
watercress, chopped
15 mL (1 tablespoon) butter

15 mL (1 tablespoon)
pimento, cooked and chopped

Method
— Pour the boiling water and
  the lemon juice into a
  casserole and add the rice;
  cover and cook at 100%
  for 5 minutes.
— Reduce the power to 70%
  and continue to cook for
  10 minutes.
— In another dish combine
  the watercress, butter and
  pimento and cook at
  100% for 1 minute.
— Combine this mixture with
  the rice and let stand for
  10 minutes before serving.

Level of Difficulty	🍴
Preparation Time	10 min
Cost per Serving	$
Number of Servings	4
Nutritional Value	115 calories 1.8 g protein 23 g carbohydrate
Food Exchanges	1/4 fruit exchange 1 bread exchange 1/2 fat exchange
Cooking Time	16 min
Standing Time	10 min
Power Level	100%, 70%
Write Your Cooking Time Here	

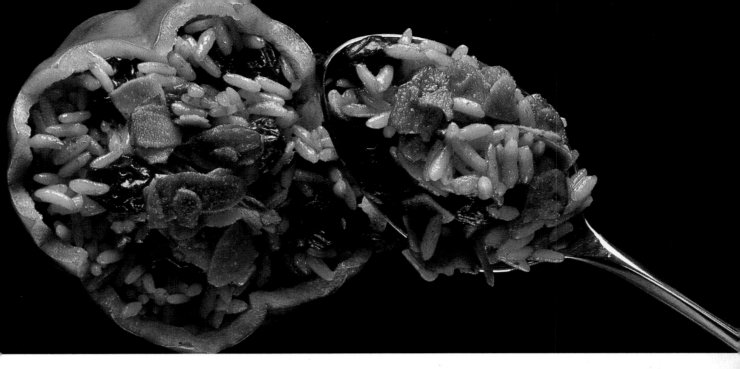

Rice with Almonds

Ingredients
250 mL (1 cup) long grain rice
500 mL (2 cups) hot beef stock
1 onion, finely chopped
15 mL (1 tablespoon) parsley, chopped
50 mL (1/4 cup) dried raisins
50 mL (1/4 cup) almonds, slivered
50 mL (1/4 cup) butter
salt and pepper to taste

Method
— In a casserole combine the rice, beef stock, onion, parsley and raisins.
— Cover and cook at 100% for 5 minutes; reduce the power to 70% and cook for 10 minutes longer.
— Let stand for 10 minutes.
— In the meantime, cook the almonds in the butter in a small dish at 100% for 2 to 3 minutes, stirring once during the cooking time.
— Combine with the rice and serve.

Level of Difficulty	🍴
Preparation Time	15 min
Cost per Serving	$
Number of Servings	4
Nutritional Value	287 calories 6.4 g protein 31 g carbohydrate
Food Exchanges	1 oz meat 1 fruit exchange 1 bread exchange 1-1/2 fat exchanges
Cooking Time	18 min
Standing Time	10 min
Power Level	100%, 70%
Write Your Cooking Time Here	

Rice and Lobster Salad

Level of Difficulty	🍴
Preparation Time	15 min*
Cost per Serving	$ $ $
Number of Servings	3
Nutritional Value	303 calories 13 g protein 18 g carbohydrate
Food Exchanges	1-1/2 oz meat 1 bread exchange 2 fat exchanges
Cooking Time	15 min
Standing Time	None
Power Level	100%, 70%
Write Your Cooking Time Here	

* The salad should be allowed to cool before serving.

Ingredients
150 mL (2/3 cup) long grain rice
375 mL (1-1/2 cups) hot fish stock
50 mL (1/4 cup) onion, chopped
15 mL (1 tablespoon) lemon zest, grated
250 mL (1 cup) lobster meat, cooked
75 mL (1/3 cup) celery, diced
75 mL (1/3 cup) yellow pepper, chopped

Vinaigrette:
50 mL (1/4 cup) oil
15 mL (1 tablespoon) vinegar
5 mL (1 teaspoon) Dijon mustard
pepper to taste

Method
— In a casserole, combine the rice, fish stock, onion and lemon zest; cover and cook at 100% for 5 minutes.
— Reduce the power to 70% and cook for 10 minutes longer. Allow to cool.
— Prepare the vinaigrette by blending the oil, vinegar, Dijon mustard and pepper.
— When ready to serve, place portions of the rice mixtures on individual salad plates, make a small well in the center of each and fill with lobster meat.
— Garnish with the diced celery and yellow pepper and pour some of the vinaigrette over each salad.

Indian Rice

Level of Difficulty	
Preparation Time	20 min
Cost per Serving	$
Number of Servings	4
Nutritional Value	275 calories 19 g protein 22 g carbohydrate
Food Exchanges	2 oz meat 1 bread exchange 1 fat exchange
Cooking Time	22 min
Standing Time	None
Power Level	100%, 70%
Write Your Cooking Time Here	

Ingredients
250 mL (1 cup) long grain rice
500 mL (2 cups) boiling fish stock
30 mL (2 tablespoons) butter
1 onion, chopped
2 hard-boiled eggs
225 g (8 oz) cooked fish fillets
2 mL (1/2 teaspoon) cayenne pepper
5 mL (1 teaspoon) celery salt
salt and pepper to taste

Method
— Put the rice in a dish and add the fish stock; cover and cook at 100% for 5 minutes.
— Reduce the power to 70%, continue to cook for 10 minutes and set aside.
— Cook the butter and chopped onion at 100% for 2 to 3 minutes, stirring once during the cooking time.
— Remove the yolks from the hard-boiled eggs and pass through a sieve, chop the egg whites and set both aside.
— Add the fish fillets to the cooked rice, stir in the egg whites and the cooked onions and mix well.
— Add the cayenne, celery salt, salt, pepper; heat at 70% for 3 to 4 minutes, stirring once during the cooking time.
— Garnish with the sieved egg yolks before serving.

First assemble the ingredients needed for this recipe, one that offers a unique way to prepare rice.

Remove the yolks from the hard-boiled eggs and pass them through a sieve. Chop the egg whites.

Add the fish fillets to the cooked rice, stir in the egg whites and onions and mix well.

Rice and Vegetable Casserole

Level of Difficulty	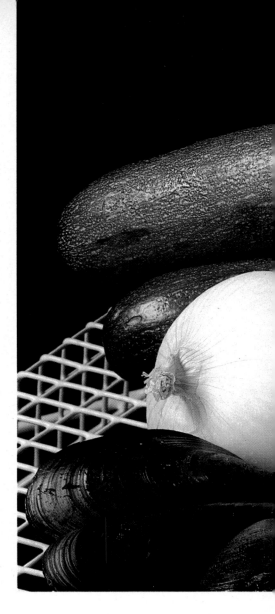
Preparation Time	30 min
Cost per Serving	$
Number of Servings	4
Nutritional Value	494 calories 27 g protein 70 g carbohydrate
Food Exchanges	3 oz meat 1 vegetable exchange 2 bread exchanges 1 fat exchange
Cooking Time	20 min
Standing Time	10 min
Power Level	100%, 70%
Write Your Cooking Time Here	

Ingredients
250 mL (1 cup) long grain rice
4 small potatoes, peeled and sliced
4 tomatoes, peeled and sliced
2 zucchini, sliced
6 small onions, sliced
450 g (1 lb) cooked mussels
90 g (3 oz) breadcrumbs
90 g (3 oz) Parmesan cheese, grated
30 mL (2 tablespoons) melted butter
1 clove garlic, crushed
500 mL (2 cups) hot chicken stock

Method
— In a casserole layer half the rice, potatoes, tomatoes, zucchini, onions, mussels, breadcrumbs and Parmesan and sprinkle with 15 mL (1 tablespoon) of the melted butter.
— Repeat this operation by layering the remaining ingredients in the same way.
— Add the garlic to the hot chicken stock and pour over the mixture in the casserole.
— Cover and cook at 100% for 5 minutes.
— Reduce the power to 70% and continue to cook for 15 minutes longer.
— Let stand for 10 minutes before serving.

This delicious rice casserole is easy to make. First assemble the ingredients required.

Layer half the rice, potatoes, tomatoes, zucchini, onions, mussels, breadcrumbs and Parmesan in a casserole.

Add the garlic to the hot chicken stock and pour over the assembled dish before cooking.

Saffron Rice

Level of Difficulty	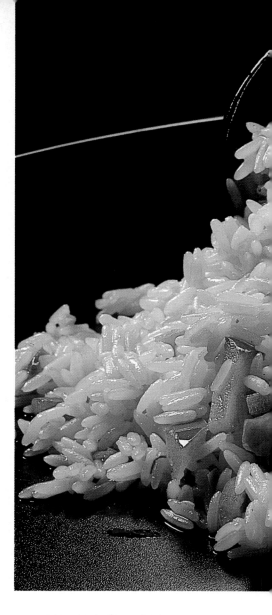
Preparation Time	10 min
Cost per Serving	$
Number of Servings	6
Nutritional Value	108 calories 1.6 g protein 18 g carbohydrate
Food Exchanges	1 bread exchange 1/2 fat exchange
Cooking Time	25 min
Standing Time	10 min
Power Level	100%, 70%
Write Your Cooking Time Here	

Ingredients
375 mL (1-1/2 cups) long grain rice
15 mL (1 tablespoon) oil
50 mL (1/4 cup) green pepper, chopped
1 clove garlic, crushed
750 mL (3 cups) hot water
1 mL (1/4 teaspoon) saffron

Method
— Put the oil into a dish and add the green pepper and garlic; cover and cook at 100% for 2 to 3 minutes.
— Add the hot water, the saffron and the rice and cover again.
— Cook at 100% for 8 minutes; reduce the power to 70% and continue to cook for 13 to 14 minutes.
— Let stand for 10 minutes before serving.

You need only a few ingredients to make this easy but tasty recipe for saffron rice.

MICROTIPS

Making Risotto

The basic principle for making risotto is quite simple; the rice is cooked in an abundant amount of rich liquid to obtain a sort of thick soup held together by the starch from the rice.

To make a basic risotto, brown a finely chopped onion in butter and oil. In another dish, make a beef bouillon and keep it hot. Add the rice to the butter, oil and onion and stir well to coat the rice. Then pour the boiling bouillon over the rice and cook. Add Parmesan cheese, but always wait until the rice has finished cooking.

It is possible to vary this recipe in many ways by adding other ingredients to this basic recipe. Venetian-style risotto is made by adding ham and peas. Risotto Milanese style is made with white wine and beef marrow as complementary ingredients. Any vegetable that is in season may also be added to make a savory risotto.

Risotto Milanese Style

Level of Difficulty	
Preparation Time	15 min
Cost per Serving	$
Number of Servings	8
Nutritional Value	195 calories 8.3 g protein 21 g carbohydrate
Food Exchanges	1 oz meat 1 bread exchange 1 fat exchange
Cooking Time	32 min
Standing Time	10 min
Power Level	100%, 70%
Write Your Cooking Time Here	

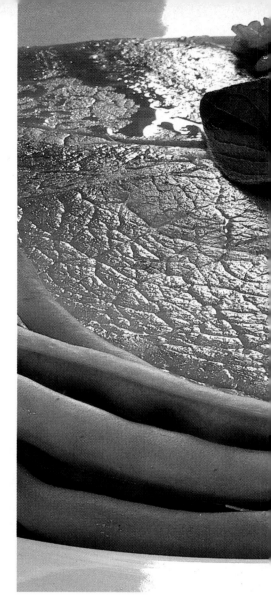

Ingredients
500 mL (2 cups) long grain rice
1 onion, chopped
50 mL (1/4 cup) beef marrow, coarsely chopped
45 mL (3 tablespoons) butter
125 mL (1/2 cup) white wine
875 mL (3-1/2 cups) hot beef stock
90 g (3 oz) Parmesan cheese, grated

Method
— Combine the onion, beef marrow and butter in a dish and cook at 100% for 4 to 5 minutes.
— Add the rice and mix well; add the white wine and beef stock and cook at 100% for 10 minutes.
— Reduce the power to 70% and cook for 15 to 17 minutes or until cooked through.
— Add the Parmesan cheese, mix well and let stand for 10 minutes before serving.

Beef marrow, combined with the other ingredients shown, gives risotto Milanese style its characteristic flavor.

MICROTIPS

Quick Rice with Tomato Juice

When you are pressed for time, precooked rice is a quick solution. It can be cooked in water or, for an interesting change, the water can be replaced with an equal amount of tomato juice. Season to taste.

Rice with Vegetable Juice

As in the preceding recipe, precooked rice can also be made with any other vegetable juice instead of water. Prepare it as above, season to taste, and in no time you will have a quick, tasty rice dish.

Rice with Orange Juice

To add an interesting touch to seafood dishes, try cooking rice in orange juice and season with an appropriate aromatic.

Rice with Chicken

Level of Difficulty	
Preparation Time	20 min
Cost per Serving	$
Number of Servings	4
Nutritional Value	354 calories 32.6 g protein 34.1 g carbohydrate
Food Exchanges	3 oz meat 1 vegetable exchange 2 bread exchanges
Cooking Time	35 min
Standing Time	12 min
Power Level	100%, 90%, 70%
Write Your Cooking Time Here	

Ingredients
375 mL (1-1/2 cups) long grain rice
30 mL (2 tablespoons) butter
1 onion, finely chopped
2 mL (1/2 teaspoon) turmeric
675 mL (2-3/4 cups) hot chicken stock
450 g (1 lb) chicken breasts, boned and skinned
1 clove garlic, crushed
30 mL (2 tablespoons) lemon juice
2 tomatoes, coarsely chopped
1 small green pepper, cut into strips

Method
— Put the butter and onion in a dish and cook at 100% for 2 to 3 minutes, stirring once during the cooking time.
— Add the rice, turmeric and hot chicken stock; cover and cook at 100% for 8 minutes.
— Reduce the power to 70% and continue to cook for 12 to 14 minutes.
— Let stand for 10 minutes.
— In the meantime, cut the chicken breast meat into strips.
— Put the chicken into a dish and add garlic and lemon juice; cover and cook at 90% for 5 to 6 minutes, stirring twice during the cooking time.
— Add the cooked chicken, tomatoes and green pepper to the cooked rice; cover and cook at 70% for 3 to 4 minutes.
— Let stand for 2 minutes before serving.

*These ingredients are all you
need to make this inexpensive
and tasty dish.*

*Cut the chicken breast meat
into even strips and cook with
the garlic and lemon juice.*

*Add the cooked chicken,
tomatoes and green pepper
strips to the cooked rice dish
and heat through.*

Chicken and Rice Vol-au-Vents

Level of Difficulty	🍴
Preparation Time	20 min
Cost per Serving	$
Number of Servings	6
Nutritional Value	390 calories 12.7 g protein 23.2 g carbohydrate
Food Exchanges	1 oz meat 1/4 milk exchange 2 bread exchanges 3 fat exchanges
Cooking Time	13 min
Standing Time	None
Power Level	100%
Write Your Cooking Time Here	

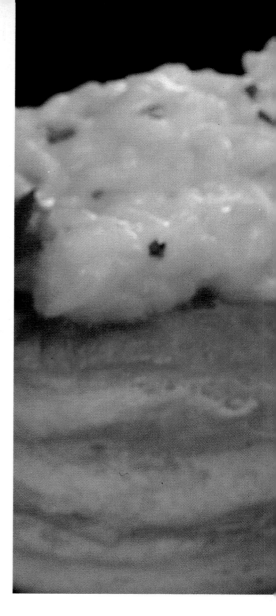

Ingredients
250 mL (1 cup) chicken, cooked and cubed
125 mL (1/2 cup) rice, cooked
45 mL (3 tablespoons) butter
50 mL (1/4 cup) onion, finely chopped
45 mL (3 tablespoons) flour
250 mL (1 cup) milk
250 mL (1 cup) chicken stock
salt and pepper to taste
15 mL (1 tablespoon) parsley, chopped
15 mL (1 tablespoon) red pepper, roasted and chopped
6 pastry shells

Method
— Put the butter and onion into a dish and cook at 100% for 2 minutes, stirring once during the cooking time.
— Add the flour and mix well; blend in the milk, chicken stock, salt and pepper; cook at 100% for 6 to 8 minutes, stirring every 2 minutes.
— Add the parsley, red pepper, cooked rice and chicken to the sauce and mix well.
— Heat at 100% for 2 to 3 minutes, stirring every minute.
— Pour the mixture into the pastry shells and serve immediately.

Whether for a a family supper or a small dinner party, vol-au-vents are always well received. These are the ingredients needed to prepare this recipe.

Put the butter and onion in a dish and cook at 100% for 2 minutes.

Add the flour, the liquid ingredients and the seasoning; stir the sauce every 2 minutes to keep it smooth and creamy.

Add the remaining ingredients to the sauce before the final stage of cooking.

Entertaining

Menu:
Cream of Carrot Soup
Brown Rice and Mushroom Salad
Veal Scallopini with Cream
Chestnut Mousse

Classic! That's the best way to describe the menu we are offering here. Although conceived to please everyone's taste, it is dedicated to gourmets who enjoy great culinary traditions. Featuring the aromas and flavors of old Italy, this menu is appropriate for any special occasion but it is certainly suitable for a quiet, intimate evening meal as well.

To introduce the meal, a rich and smooth cream of carrot soup is served. Made with a flavorful meat broth and gently simmered, it sets the tone for the remainder of the meal.

All your guests will enjoy the brown rice and mushroom salad. In this recipe the rice is not cooked in water but in a rich vegetable broth, which gives it a very special flavor. This traditional salad, garnished with onions and mushrooms, is usually served with a light vinaigrette.

For the main course, a delicate and flavorful veal

scallopini is served with succulent fettuccine—a classic dish that should please the most refined palate.

And to complete this feast, we suggest a chestnut mousse. A classic menu for an evening of entertaining!

From the Recipe to Your Table

Planning a meal for a number of friends or family is hard work and requires a certain amount of organization. Cooking a complete meal in the microwave oven must be planned ahead in the same way as cooking a meal in a conventional oven. Only the cooking and reheating times vary.

Order of preparation:
24 hours before the meal:
— Prepare the cream of carrot soup and soak the chestnuts.
8 hours before the meal:
— Prepare the chestnut mousse.
5 hours before the meal:
— Prepare the brown rice and mushroom salad.
40 minutes before the meal:
— Prepare the fettuccine and the veal scallopini.

98

Cream of Carrot Soup

Ingredients
900 g (2 lb) carrots, grated
50 mL (1/4 cup) butter
1 onion, chopped
4 cloves garlic, crushed
1.75 L (7 cups) chicken stock
125 mL (1/2 cup) 35% cream
10 mL (2 teaspoons) sugar
salt and pepper to taste
parsley, chopped

Method
— Melt the butter in a dish at
  100% for 1 minute.
— Add the carrots, onion and
  garlic and mix well; cover
  and cook at 100% for 4 to
  5 minutes, stirring once
  during the cooking time.
— Stir the mixture and add
  the chicken stock.
— Cover again and cook at
  100% for 1 hour, stirring
  once during the cooking
  time.
— Pour into a blender and
  blend at high speed for
  several seconds, until
  creamy.
— Add the cream and sugar
  and season to taste.
— Refrigerate until ready to
  serve.
— Sprinkle with parsley
  before serving.

Note: This soup can be
thinned with more chicken
stock if necessary.

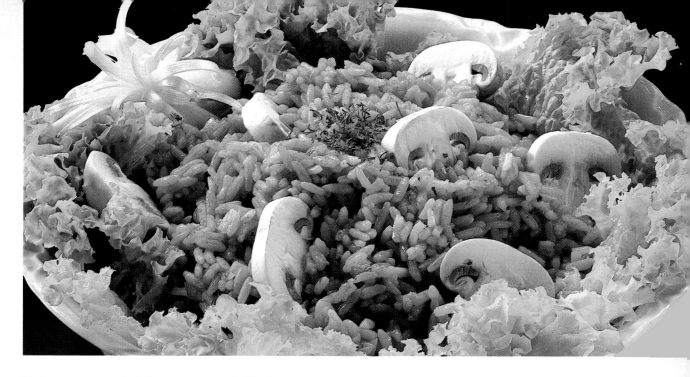

Brown Rice and Mushroom Salad

Ingredients
250 mL (1 cup) long grain
brown rice
15 mL (1 tablespoon) butter
1 onion, finely chopped
500 mL (2 cups) hot vegetable
broth
450 g (1 lb) mushrooms,
thinly sliced

Vinaigrette:
90 mL (3 oz) oil
30 mL (1 oz) vinegar
salt and pepper to taste

Method
— Put the butter and onion in
a dish and cook at 100%
for 2 to 3 minutes, stirring
once during the cooking
time.
— Add the rice and the hot
vegetable broth; cover
and cook at 100% for 5
minutes.
— Reduce the power to 70%
and continue to cook for
25 to 30 minutes.
— Allow to cool.
— Add the mushrooms and
set aside.
— To prepare the vinaigrette,
blend the oil with the
vinegar, salt and pepper.
— Pour the vinaigrette over
the salad before serving.

Veal Scallopini with Cream

Level of Difficulty	🍴🍴
Preparation Time	15 min
Cost per Serving	$ $
Number of Servings	4
Nutritional Value	561 calories 33.6 g protein 35 g carbohydrate
Food Exchanges	3 oz meat 2 bread exchanges 1/4 milk exchange 3 fat exchanges
Cooking Time	29 min
Standing Time	None
Power Level	100%, 70%, 50%
Write Your Cooking Time Here	

Ingredients
4 veal escallops
225 g (8 oz) fettuccine
1 L (4 cups) water
5 mL (1 teaspoon) salt
5 mL (1 teaspoon) oil
30 mL (2 tablespoons) butter
15 mL (1 tablespoon) flour
250 mL (1 cup) 18% cream
15 mL (1 tablespoon) lemon juice
pepper to taste

Method
— Pour the water into a dish and bring to the boil by heating at 100% for 9 to 10 minutes; add the salt, oil and the fettuccine.
— Cover the dish and cook the fettuccine at 100% for 5 to 7 minutes, stirring twice during the cooking time.
— Drain the pasta, rinse under cold water and set aside.
— Preheat a browning dish at 100% for 7 minutes; add the butter and heat at 100% for 30 seconds.
— Sear the veal escallops.
— Reduce the power to 70% and cook the escallops for 3 to 4 minutes.
— Remove the veal and set aside.
— Add the flour to the butter and mix well.
— Blend in the cream, lemon juice and pepper and mix well; cook at 100% for 3 to 4 minutes, stirring every minute.
— Arrange the fettuccine and the veal on a microwave-safe platter and spoon the sauce over the veal escallops.
— Heat at 50% for 3 to 4 minutes before serving.

Chestnut Mousse

Ingredients
225 g (8 oz) chestnuts
50 mL (1/4 cup) water
125 mL (1/2 cup) icing sugar
30 mL (2 tablespoons) cocoa
2 mL (1/2 teaspoon) vanilla
250 mL (1 cup) 35% cream

Method
— Soak the chestnuts for about 12 hours in cold water.
— Drain the chestnuts and peel them.
— Pour 50 mL (1/4 cup) of water into a dish and add the chestnuts; cover and cook at 100% for 6 to 7 minutes, stirring once during the cooking time.
— Place the cooked chestnuts with the cooking liquid in a blender and blend at high speed for several seconds until reduced to a purée.
— Add the icing sugar, cocoa and vanilla and blend well; transfer the mixture to another bowl.
— Whip the cream with an electric hand beater and add it to the chestnut mixture.
— Pour the chestnut mousse into individual bowls and refrigerate. Garnish as desired before serving.

MICROTIPS

Saffron Rice

At some time in the past you may have been impressed by an appetizing casserole—one in which the ingredients were combined with a brilliant yellow rice. The odds are that the rice was prepared with saffron, a spice that gives it this magnificent color as well as a delicious flavor. Saffron is used in a number of traditional dishes, such as Spanish paella, and it adds character to new rice recipes.

To prepare a delicious saffron rice, first cook the rice and any vegetables suggested in the recipe. Heat 75 mL (5 tablespoons) of water with some olive oil or butter and a little saffron. Pour the hot liquid over the cooked rice, stir well and cook at 100%, without stirring, for 2 minutes.

Pasta and Rice Terminology

Like all great arts, the art of cooking has developed a specialized vocabulary over the course of its long history. The terms used may designate methods of preparation or the dishes themselves. Because you will find these terms in the recipes listed in this volume as well as in other cookbooks, we have made a list of some of the more common ones used.

Al dente: An Italian expression meaning "to the tooth." This is the traditional Italian way of designating the ideal degree of doneness for all pasta. Pasta al dente is cooked but still firm. The pasta will yield to the teeth but not to the pressure of the tongue.

Basmati rice: A small long grain rice that originates in India and has a very distinct flavor.

Cargo rice: Beige grains of rice which, historically, were husked. They can be found today with the husk on and are thus more nutritious. The name derives from the fact that cargo rice came from the Far East by boat.

Mafalda: A narrow lasagna, smaller than lasagnette, scalloped on both sides so that the scallops form a £° angle with the ribbon of pasta. This pasta was named in honor of the princess Mafalda, one of the two daughters of the Italian king Victor-Emmanuel III who reigned from 1915 to 1946. (See also Yolanda.)

Noodle: Although this term has come to be widely used in North America, it originally designated a ribbon of pasta only 1 cm wide—the Italian tagliatelle. Wider noodles, known as tagliatelle larghe or fettucce, are also available.

Parmesan: An Italian cheese that is traditionally served grated with spaghetti and with other pasta. It is made from skimmed cow milk and contains 32% fat. It has a crust and is hard, yellow and crumbly. The flavor of Parmesan is somewhat fruity and slightly sharp.

Pesto: A paste made by crushing fresh basil and garlic in a small amount of olive oil. Some recipes add pine nuts and/or cheese. Pesto originated in northern Italy and is also traditional in the Provence region of France, where it is known as *pistou*. It is frequently used to flavor pasta and may be used in soups as well.

Pilaf: This word, originating in the Middle East, designates a way of cooking rice or wheat in which the grains are heated in fat before the liquid is added. Rice cooked in this manner always separates easily. The term also applies to barley cooked in this way.

Risotto: A classic Italian rice dish, the term means "small rice." Traditional risotto is prepared by browning dry rice with a chopped onion in a mixture of butter and olive oil and then adding bouillon and stirring constantly to release as much starch as possible from the rice. Risotto is finished off with different ingredients and seasonings, which vary from region to region.

Scalloped: This term is used to describe the borders of lasagna noodles or any other pasta with curly or wavy edges.

Semolina: A granular flour made from hard durum wheat that is used to make pasta, couscous and other products found in many kinds of soup.

Yolanda: Ribbon pasta, scalloped on one side only, that is wider than fettucce but narrower than mafalda (see above). This pasta was named in honor of the princess Yolanda, one of the two daughters of the Italian king Victor-Emmanuel III who reigned from 1915 to 1946.

Culinary Terms

Have you ever been given a menu and found that you were unable to understand many of the words? Not only are there a number of culinary terms that are obscure but there are many ways to cook pasta or rice that have special terms to describe them. Here is a short glossary of terms with descriptions of their meanings that may help you.

Alla bolognese: Refers to spaghetti served with a sauce made with ground meat, tomatoes and aromatic seasoning.

Alla carbonara: Meaning "in the manner of the coal merchant," this term refers to spaghetti prepared with a sauce made from eggs, cream and bacon.

Alla genovese: Refers to tagliatelle served with a garlic-based sauce with grated Parmesan cheese, basil and fresh parsley.

Alla napoletana: Refers to spaghetti prepared with tomato sauce.

Alla valenciana: A rice pilaf cooked with diced raw ham, diced green peppers and peas.

Rice croquettes: Traditionally prepared from a risotto bound with egg yolks, and with Parmesan cheese and butter as ingredients. Frequently, the croquettes are breaded, fried and served with tomato sauce.

Risotto alla matriciana: A risotto prepared with diced salt pork, garlic and diced tomatoes.

Conversion Chart

**Conversion Chart for the
Main Measures Used in
Cooking**

Volume
1 teaspoon............ 5 mL
1 tablespoon......... 15 mL

1 quart (4 cups)....... 1 litre
1 pint (2 cups)....... 500 mL
1/2 cup............ 125 mL
1/4 cup............. 50 mL

Weight
2.2 lb.......... 1 kg (1000 g)
1.1 lb............... 500 g
0.5 lb............... 225 g
0.25 lb.............. 115 g

1 oz................. 30 g

**Metric Equivalents
for Cooking
Temperatures**

49°C.............. 120°F	120°C.............. 250°F
54°C.............. 130°F	135°C.............. 275°F
60°C.............. 140°F	150°C.............. 300°F
66°C.............. 150°F	160°C.............. 325°F
71°C.............. 160°F	180°C.............. 350°F
77°C.............. 170°F	190°C.............. 375°F
82°C.............. 180°F	200°C.............. 400°F
93°C.............. 200°F	220°C.............. 425°F
107°C.............. 225°F	230°C.............. 450°F

Readers will note that, in the recipes, we give 250 mL as the equivalent for 1 cup and 450 g as the equivalent for 1 lb and that fractions of these measurements are even less mathematically accurate. The reason for this is that mathematically accurate conversions are just not practical in cooking. Your kitchen scales are simply not accurate enough to weigh 454 g—the true equivalent of 1 lb—and it would be a waste of time to try. The conversions given in this series, therefore, necessarily represent approximate equivalents, but they will still give excellent results in the kitchen. No problems should be encountered if you adhere to either metric or imperial measurements throughout a recipe.

Index

B

Be Your Own Pasta Chef! 42
Brown Rice and Mushroom
   Salad 101

C

Cannelloni with Veal and
   Spinach 50
Chestnut Mousse 105
Chicken and Rice
   Vol-au-Vents 96
Classic Lasagna 34
Conversion Chart 109
Cooking Pasta 18
Cream of Carrot Soup 100
Culinary Terms 108

E

Entertaining 98
  — Brown Rice and Mushroom
     Salad 101
  — Chestnut Mousse 105
  — Cream of Carrot Soup 100
  — Veal Scallopini with
     Cream 104

F

Fettuccine with Red Wine 45
Fettuccine with Roquefort
   Cheese 46
Freezing and Defrosting Pasta . . . 19
Fried Rice with Shrimp 70

G

Gnocchi with Cream 64
Guide to Pasta, A 10

H

How to Make Fettuccine 44
How to Make Ravioli 52

I

Indian Rice 86

L

Lasagna 32
Lasagna with Four Cheeses 38
Lasagna with Salmon 40
Lemon Rice 82
Linguine with Mushrooms
   and Cream 62

M

Macaroni with Cheddar
   Cheese 61
Manicotti with Pike 53

N

Note from the Editor 6

P

Pasta Parade, A 12
Pasta and Rice Terminology 106
Pasta Filled with a Surprise 48
Pasta, Rice, and the
   Microwave Oven 8
Power Levels 7

R

Ravioli in Soup 56
Ravioli with Scallops and
   Fennel 58
Rice and Lobster Salad 84
Rice—An Underrated Staple 66
Rice and Vegetable Casserole 88
Rice and Orange Stuffing 80
Rice and Vegetable Stuffing 78
Rice Pilaf 68
Rice Quiche 74
Rice with Almonds 83
Rice with Chicken 94
Rice with Pork and Vegetables . . . 76
Risotto Milanese Style 92

S

Saffron Rice 90
Spaghetti—A Universal Pasta . . . 20
Spaghetti Carbonara 24
Spaghetti with Meatballs and
   Tomato Sauce 22
Spaghetti with Tuna Sauce 28
Spaghetti with Clam Sauce 26
Spaghettini with Garlic 30
Spinach and Veal Filling 52
Spinach Lasagna Bolognese 36
Storing Pasta 17

T

Table of Contents 5
Tortellini with Cream 54

U

Utensils for Cooking Pasta 16
Utensils for Making Pasta 14

V

Veal Scallopini with Cream 104

W

Wild Rice 72

MICROTIPS

Use Cheese Instead of
   Butter and Salt 27
Pasta and Cheese 31
Which Cheese to Choose? . . . 38
Pasta with a Splendid
   Yellow Color 57
Keeping Grated Cheese
   on Hand 60
To Cook Cannelloni and
   Lasagna Quickly 60
Using a Variety of
   Cheeses 60
Cooking Times for Rice 69
Use Leftover Rice
   in Soups 73
Freezing and Defrosting
   Leftover Rice 77
For Fluffy Rice 79
Making Croquettes or Rice
   Pudding 81
Making Risotto 91
Quick Rice with Tomato
   Juice 93
Rice with Vegetable Juice . . . 93
Rice with Orange Juice 93
Saffron Rice 105